100% of the royalties from this book are being
donated to Catholic Charities USA

"A triumph! One of the best presentations of the Church's social teaching. Brandon Vogt adeptly and correctly positions social justice in relation to the lives of the saints, and in doing so he rescues it from the ideological constraints that have for far too long made this essential teaching of the Church inaccessible to most of the faithful. Social justice is not simply a theory, but a whole way of life, revealed in all its radical and saving grace in the lives of the Church's saints."

—**Very Reverend Robert E. Barron**, Rector of Mundelein Seminary and founder of Word on Fire Catholic Ministries

"A much-needed, well-written, and always-inspiring book. Brandon Vogt reminds us that "social justice" is not a dirty word; rather, it's firmly rooted in the Gospels, in the church's social teachings, and, as he artfully shows us, in the lives of the great heroes and heroines of our faith. This timely book reminds us that we are called not simply to care for the poor, but to work against anything that would keep them poor. The saints — and Jesus — would want no less from us."

— **James Martin, S.J.**, author of *Jesus: A Pilgrimage*

"In this book, Brandon Vogt situates the principles of Catholic social teaching within the venerable Catholic spiritual tradition by presenting these principles within the details of the actual lives of the saints. Each description becomes as vivid as a stained-glass window as it illustrates how each saint lived out the Gospel, and then it presents us with concrete lessons we can use today. This presentation will easily lead the reader to reflection and then to action. I highly recommend Saints and Social Justice *as a rich resource for your spiritual reading."*

— **Rev. Larry Snyder**, President of Catholic Charities USA

"Incredibly accessible: Brandon Vogt brings Catholic social teaching to life through the actions and examples of the saints. As we cannot commit to what we do not understand, this book opens minds and hearts to connect faith with personal action. An indispensable teaching resource!

— **Dr. Carolyn Woo**, President and CEO of Catholic Relief Services

"Somebody has described the social teaching of the Catholic Church as its best-kept secret. Brandon Vogt has done a great job letting this immense cat of common sense, divine revelation, and liberating truth and love out of the bag and setting it on the scurrying mice of lies, oppression, and cruelty that are nibbling away at the foundations of our civilization. May his tribe increase!"

— **Mark P. Shea**, author of *Salt and Light: The Commandments, the Beatitudes, and a Joyful Life*

"With Saints and Social Justice: A Guide to Changing the World, *author Brandon Vogt dares to suggest that our world might be saved from its "either/or" self by the non-ideological "both/and" that has always been Catholic social teaching. Intent on bringing those dread words "social justice" into the light and rescuing them from rhetorical misuse, Vogt cites the disparate lives and works of Mother Teresa of Calcutta, Dorothy Day, St. John Paul II, St. Thomas More, and others, to illustrate just how completely our perceived "sides" and ideologies disappear when issues of life, family, rights, poverty, and human dignity are addressed through the Christ-centered lenses of justice and mercy. This is an accessible book, and a brave one, too. It trusts that we want to leave a better and more peaceable world to our children than the stale-mated, divided one we currently inhabit."

— **Elizabeth Scalia**, author of *Strange Gods: Unmasking the Idols in our Everyday Lives* and the blogger known as The Anchoress

"Brandon Vogt's newest book offers us a fresh view on Catholic social doctrine from the Church's best and clearest thinkers: the saints. Vogt takes up Francis Cardinal George's challenge to set aside partisan ideologies and propose Catholic social doctrine in a "simply Catholic" manner. Vogt's clear, engaging, and accessible style of writing, combined with the practical wisdom of saints who lived these ethical principles out in the real world, with all its ambiguities and challenges, makes Vogt's book an excellent introduction to the topic and can be used as a resource for personal reflection, teen or adult group study, or RCIA."

— **Dr. Thomas Neal**, Professor of Spiritual Theology and Academic Dean at Notre Dame Seminary in New Orleans, Louisiana

"The social teachings of the Catholic Church often produce tension or debate. But in this book, Brandon Vogt provides us the opportunity to pray these teachings through, seeing and experiencing them through the lives of the saints. This engaging and well-written work will you help you understand them anew in fresh ways."

— **Rev. Msgr. Charles Pope**, blogger and priest in the Archdiocese of Washington

SAINTS AND SOCIAL JUSTICE

A GUIDE TO CHANGING THE WORLD

BRANDON VOGT

Our Sunday Visitor Publishing Division
Our Sunday Visitor, Inc.
Huntington, Indiana 46750

Nihil Obstat:
Msgr. Michael Heintz, Ph.D.
Censor Librorum

Imprimatur:
✠ Kevin C. Rhoades
Bishop of Fort Wayne-South Bend
December 20, 2013

The *Nihil Obstat* and *Imprimatur* are
declarations that a work is free from
doctrinal or moral error. It is not implied
that those who have granted the *Nihil Obstat*
and *Imprimatur* agree with the contents,
opinions, or statements expressed.

Copyright © 2014 by Brandon Vogt.
Published 2014.

20 19 18 17 16 15   2 3 4 5 6 7 8 9

ISBN 978-1-61278-690-2
(Inventory No. T1395)
eISBN: 978-1-61278-341-3
LCCN: 2014936797

Cover and interior design: Lindsey Riesen
Cover photos: Mother Teresa with a baby,
Dinodia / The Bridgeman Art Library; Pope
John Paul II on his way to Mass at Heaton
Park, Manchester, Monday, May 31, 1982,
Spencer/Mirrorpix/Newscom; Dorothy Day,
Marquette University Archives.

Interior photos: p. 18, The Bridgeman Art
Library; p. 28, The Crosiers; p. 39, The
Crosiers; p. 47, Claudio Giovanni Colombo
/ Shutterstock.com; p. 57, Wikimedia; p.
66, The Crosiers; p. 77, File photo; p. 86,
The Crosiers; p. 97, The Crosiers; p. 106,
Marquette University Archives; p. 117,
Spencer/Mirrorpix/Newscom; p. 126, File
photo; p. 136, The Crosiers; p. 143, The
Crosiers.

PRINTED IN THE UNITED STATES
OF AMERICA

TO ISAIAH MARTIN VOGT

May you follow your namesakes and "bring good news to the afflicted, bind up the brokenhearted, and proclaim liberty to the captives," and remember that "injustice anywhere is a threat to justice everywhere."

"No one can demand that religion should be relegated to the inner sanctum of personal life, without influence on societal and national life…. An authentic faith — which is never comfortable or completely personal — **always involves a deep desire to change the world**, to transmit values, to leave this earth somehow better that we found it."

— Pope Francis[1]

CONTENTS

Foreword *by Archbishop J. Peter Sartain* 10
Introduction 14

LIFE AND DIGNITY OF THE HUMAN PERSON 17
Chapter 1 — Bl. Teresa of Calcutta 18
Chapter 2 — St. Peter Claver 28

CALL TO FAMILY, COMMUNITY, AND PARTICIPATION 38
Chapter 3 — St. Frances of Rome 39
Chapter 4 — Bl. Anne Marie Javouhey 47

RIGHTS AND RESPONSIBILITIES 56
Chapter 5 — St. Roque González 57
Chapter 6 — St. Thomas More 66

OPTION FOR THE POOR AND VULNERABLE 76
Chapter 7 — Bl. Pier Giorgio Frassati 77
Chapter 8 — St. Vincent de Paul 86

THE DIGNITY OF WORK AND THE RIGHTS OF WORKERS 96
Chapter 9 — St. Benedict of Nursia 97
Chapter 10 — Servant of God Dorothy Day 106

SOLIDARITY 116
Chapter 11 — St. John Paul II 117
Chapter 12 — St. Damien of Molokai 126

CARE FOR CREATION 135
Chapter 13 — St. Giles 136
Chapter 14 — St. Isidore the Farmer 143

Suggested Reading 150
Acknowledgments 151
Notes 152

FOREWORD

It is one of the great ironies of our age — the *information* age, the *communications* age — that more and more people feel isolated and alone. The mind-blowing speed with which information flows, accurately or inaccurately, belies a devastating fragmentation that often disregards the human person. The superficiality of communication depersonalizes others and reduces them to objects of fascination, grist for the rumor mill. At a time when technology is being put increasingly at the service of the human family, members of that family increasingly feel left out.

In this often impersonal environment, the Church makes a salutary proposal, the proclamation of the Gospel. Since her essential mission is to evangelize, her outreach is always at the same time both personal and communal: to invite all persons into communion with the living God and with one another. That communion, moreover, is not private or static: its social aspect constantly flows beyond itself in love to all creation, particularly where there is poverty and human suffering. Rooted in God's self-revelation through Christ, the Church's social teaching begins with a premise that challenges an incomplete, superficial anthropology: she proclaims the profound dignity of every human person, created by God in his own image and likeness, and the destiny of every person for union with God. As St. John Paul II writes in *Pastores Dabo Vobis*:

> "People need to come out of their anonymity and fear. They need to be known and called by name, to walk in safety along the paths of life, to be found again if they have become lost, to be loved, to receive salvation as the supreme gift of God's love. All this is done by Jesus, the Good Shepherd...." (82)

Whereas the modern world offers fragmentation, Catholic social teaching offers integration and communion.

> "Christian revelation contributes greatly to the promotion of ... communion between persons, and at the same time leads us to a deeper understanding of the laws of social life which the Creator has written into man's spiritual and moral nature." (*Gaudium et Spes* 23)

"The Church receives from the Gospel the full revelation of the truth about man. When she fulfills her mission of proclaiming the Gospel, she bears witness to man, in the name of Christ, to his dignity and his vocation to the communion of persons. She teaches him the demands of justice and peace in conformity with divine wisdom." (CCC 2419)

"All of this is done by Jesus," St. John Paul reminds us. At its core, the Church's social teaching is irrevocably rooted in the Lord and salvation as the supreme gift of his tender love. Thus, that teaching is at the same time a *mission*, the mission of every baptized person to believe, live, and proclaim the Gospel. When uprooted from the Lord, or when sanitized into mere social theory, that mission ceases to be salt and light.

When lived by Christians as an act of faith, discipleship, devotion, and proclamation, however, the Church's social mission shines as an extraordinary light in the world. That is precisely the insight that Brandon Vogt offers in these pages. Observing that Catholic social teaching is often underappreciated and misunderstood because it has sometimes been disconnected from a relationship with Christ in the Church, Vogt suggests that "it's time to reclaim Catholic social teaching. My goal with this book is to re-introduce this body of wisdom to a world that has forgotten, misunderstood, or ignored it by unveiling these teachings through the lives of the saints.... Catholic social teaching should be well-known, well-understood, and, most of all, well-practiced."

Vogt demonstrates how the social mission of the church has been practiced from the beginning by those who have understood that genuine faith naturally flowers into love. The love and devotion to the Lord demonstrated in the lives of the saints reveals how the search for holiness never isolates one from the world; rather, those who love the Lord and nurture their relationship with him realize unmistakably that he sends them into the world as his ambassadors and instruments. This is true even of those called to life in the cloister. St. Thérèse of Lisieux, for example, who never left her Carmelite monastery, is the co-patron (with St. Francis Xavier) of missionaries and missions! In other words, communion with the Lord leads to deeper communion with all those loved by the Lord, especially the poor and suffering. That is the heart of Catholic social teaching.

In the lives of the saints chosen by Vogt, we see the integration and communion for which people hunger in our day. The integrity of the lives of the saints emerges clearly as a sign of their communion with God in prayer and the sacraments, especially the Eucharist, and in their willing surrender to the cross of Christ. Without exception, they experienced the cross in very personal ways: hardships of a wide variety, rejection, setbacks and disappointment, illness, separation, alienation, isolation, ridicule, and loneliness. In the midst of their trials, they also experienced the grace of communion with God and others through prayer, friendship, marriage, and religious community. The saints brought to life in this book understood that the call to discipleship is a call to conversion, repentance, and humility, and they bear the fruits of lives led by the Holy Spirit: love, joy, peace, patience, kindness, generosity, faithfulness, gentleness, and self-control (see Galatians 5:22).

An important principle in the Church's teaching on social justice is solidarity. Human solidarity is a reflection of our common origin in the one God and is a direct demand of human and Christian brotherhood. It is manifest by proper social ordering of the human community in work, care for the poor and sick, reconciliation of conflicts, communion among people of all social classes and nations, respect for the rights of workers, and comprehensive efforts for peace among all people. However, its roots are entirely spiritual.

"None of us lives for oneself, and no one dies for oneself," writes St. Paul (Rom 14:7). "If one part suffers, all the parts suffer with it; if one part is honored, all the parts share its joy. Now you are Christ's body, and individually parts of it" (1 Cor 12:26–27). The Church always understands the demands of solidarity in their spiritual context, for human solidarity is founded on the communion of saints. The Christian, in working for justice and peace, is to ground this activity in its relation to the sharing of the spiritual goods of the faith. "In spreading the spiritual goods of the faith, the Church has promoted, and often opened new paths for, the development of temporal goods as well" (CCC 1942), and thus verified the Lord's own words, "But seek first the kingdom of God and his righteousness, and all these things will be given you besides" (Mt 6:33).

In a discourse on June 1, 1941, Pope Pius XII remarked:

"For two thousand years this sentiment has lived and endured in the soul of the Church, impelling souls then and now to the heroic charity of monastic farmers, liberators of slaves, healers of the sick, and messengers of faith, civilization, and science to all generations and all peoples for the sake of creating the social conditions capable of offering to everyone possible a life worthy of man and of a Christian."

In these pages, readers will find a rich field of inspiration for their own hunger for justice, their own striving for peace. Saints, fellow pilgrims, and witnesses to the Lord will show them the way and strengthen their resolve to be devoted to the Lord in deep prayer and sacrificial love. This has been the call of every Christian from the very beginning, and ever will it be.

Archbishop J. Peter Sartain, D.D., S.T.L.

Seattle, Washingon

INTRODUCTION

On March 2, 2010, Glenn Beck, a popular television commentator, issued a warning to his millions of followers. He suggested that if your church uses the phrase "social justice," you should be worried:

"I beg you, look for the words 'social justice' or 'economic justice' on your church website. If you find it, run as fast as you can. Social justice and economic justice, they are code words. Now, am I advising people to leave their church? Yes!... If you have a priest that is pushing social justice, go find another parish. Go alert your bishop and tell them, 'Excuse me are you down with this whole social justice thing?' I don't care what the church is.... [I]f they say, 'Yeah, we're all in that social justice thing,' I'm in the wrong place."[2]

I had mixed emotions when I first read these comments. On the one hand, I knew how the phrase "social justice" had been co-opted to mask all sorts of nefarious projects. I also knew, as a Catholic, how the Church's social teachings had been twisted and misunderstood. Depending on who you talk with, Catholic social teaching is either too liberal, too conservative, too outdated, too modern, too idealistic, too political, or in some cases all of the above.

Yet while I understood Beck's concern, his words deeply worried me. He warned about finding "social justice" or "economic justice" on your church's website, but those exact phrases appear no less than 115 times on the Vatican's website, in the Church's official teachings and texts. Likewise, I knew if I asked bishops, priests, nuns, laypeople, and especially saints up and down the centuries whether they were "down with this whole social justice thing," their answer would be an unequivocal, "Yes."

So how did we end up here? How did Catholic social teaching develop such a bad and confused reputation? First of all, the teachings are admittedly diffuse. Although the *Compendium of the Social Doctrine of the Church* (2004) provided something close to a comprehensive summary, there's no single, magisterial source that describes it in full. These social teachings branch out from Biblical principles, papal writings, conciliar documents, episcopal statements, mystical prayer, saintly wisdom, and much more, which makes it difficult to determine what it does and does not include.

Second, these teachings can often be abstract. They have great traction in ivory towers and among intellectuals, but they're sometimes ignored by the ordinary Catholic looking for more practical spiritual advice.

Finally, these teachings have been abused. This is what Beck was getting at and his concerns are not completely without merit. The Church's teachings on justice, charity, compassion, and peace have been hijacked and misrepresented over several years. Even within the Church, different factions over- or under-emphasize certain parts, whether that be the so-called "life" issues for some or the "peace-and-justice" issues for others.

For all these reasons and more, it's time to reclaim Catholic social teaching. My goal with this book is to re-introduce this body of wisdom to a world that has forgotten, misunderstood, or ignored it by unveiling these teachings through the lives of the saints. The book is framed using the seven major themes of Catholic social teaching, as defined by the U.S. bishops, and for each theme I highlight two saints who especially embodied it.

Inside this book you'll find colorful and inspiring stories from saints who have put these teachings into action. They didn't just believe it, they lived it. As theologian Fr. Charles Fell observed: "The lives of the saints are nothing less than the law of God reduced to practice."[3]

My hope is that this book imitates stained glass windows, using the saints as conduits of light through which the radiance of Catholic social teaching can shine with new vividness and splendor.

A couple preliminary notes before diving in. First, I use the term "social justice" in the book, and in the title, as it's most popularly understood. Pope Francis used it this way in his exhortation, *Evangelii Gaudium*, when he stated that "none of us can think we are exempt from concern for the poor and for social justice."[4] Catholic social teaching typically assigns a more precise and technical meaning to that phrase, but I'm using it more generally to mean the public demands of love, justice, and charity.

Second, because I'm mainly interested in illustrating these teachings in concrete ways through the lives of the saints, I don't spend much time on abstract theory. I want to *show* rather than teach Catholic social teaching, for I agree with Pope Paul VI's observation: "Modern man listens more willingly to witnesses than to teachers, and if he does listen to teachers, it is because they are witnesses."[5] If you'd like to go deeper into the theory behind Catholic social teaching, you'll find a Suggested Reading list at the end of the book.

It's an unfortunate fact that people describe this body of wisdom as "Catholicism's best kept secret." It's time to end that. Catholic social teaching should be well-known, well-understood, and, most of all, well-practiced. The saints knew this best and so it's to them we turn.

LIFE AND DIGNITY
OF THE HUMAN PERSON

The Catholic Church proclaims that human life is sacred and that the dignity of the human person is the foundation of a moral vision for society. **This belief is the foundation of all the principles of our social teaching.** In our society, human life is under direct attack from abortion and euthanasia. The value of human life is being threatened by cloning, embryonic stem cell research, and the use of the death penalty. The intentional targeting of civilians in war or terrorist attacks is always wrong. Catholic teaching also calls on us to work to avoid war. Nations must protect the right to life by finding increasingly effective ways to prevent conflicts and resolve them by peaceful means. We believe that every person is precious, that people are more important than things, and that the measure of every institution is whether it threatens or enhances the life and dignity of the human person.[6]

CHAPTER 1
BL. TERESA
OF CALCUTTA

Sometime during my college years, I began meeting with a group of homeless men and women at a local lake. I'd visit them once or twice a week, usually with food in hand, and we'd chat for hours about life, faith, football, and whether flight or invisibility was the better superpower. But one day, as we sat at our picnic table, a strange man walked up whom I had never seen before. He looked tired and disheveled, probably homeless, and he sat down directly across from me. He stared but said nothing.

I wanted to break the ice, so I extended my hand and said, "Hi, I'm Brandon!" But again, nothing. He just sat there, stoic, unmoving, staring deep into my eyes. Finally, after about ten seconds of awkward silence, he bellowed out of the blue: "MY NAME IS JESUS CHRIST AND I DIED FOR YOUR SINS!"

I didn't know what to say. That wasn't quite the response I had expected. I sat for a few more seconds, stunned. But then he continued: "Aw, I'm just playing with you. My name's Jimmy."

After that strange and confusing introduction, we hit it off pretty well and had a great conversation. But I remember driving home that day, reflecting on the exchange, and thinking how true Jimmy's words actually were. One of my favorite biblical passages is in Matthew 25, where Jesus identified himself with the poor and marginalized. "Whatever you did for one of these least brothers of mine," Jesus explained, "you did for me."

Though Jimmy thought he was only joking, his words rang with deep and lasting truth. Sitting across from me at that picnic table, he really *was* Jesus in a mysterious sense, because Christ identifies precisely with people like Jimmy — those without jobs, without hope, and without anyone to talk to. That day he helped me glimpse an important truth, that every person carries within their soul the *imago Dei* — the image of God. What Jimmy revealed, however, a small, vivacious nun would help me see with much sharper clarity.

> ## ATHEISTS INDEED
>
> "Those who cannot see Christ in the poor are atheists indeed."
>
> — Dorothy Day[7]

THE WOMAN IN THE STREET

In the summer of 1948, as Sister Teresa wandered the streets of Calcutta, the stifling heat tempted her to return home. The convent was nice and cool, and she wasn't even sure what she was doing in the streets.

But then she spotted a woman lying in the road. The woman was half-eaten by rats and ants. She looked almost dead. People passed by on either side, few taking notice.

Yet the small Albanian nun walked over and carefully lifted the woman, cradling her like a precious work of art. It was the first time she had touched someone in the street. The nun carried her to a nearby hospital, and when the attendants saw the woman, they apologized and said there was nothing they could do; she was beyond saving. But Sister wouldn't accept that. She refused to leave until they gave the woman a bed, and after much bickering, the hospital staff finally relented. The obstinate nun got her way, as would become her custom in the following years, and helped the woman die with dignity.

What prompted this remarkable nun to help that woman in the street? The answer lies on a small train two years earlier. On September 10, 1946, Sister Teresa of Loreto traveled from Calcutta to Darjeeling for her annual spiritual retreat. With the Himalayans passing by her window she sat and prayed quietly. Suddenly, she felt jolted by an interior summons:

"I clearly felt a call within my calling. The message was very clear. I had to leave the convent and consecrate myself to helping the poor by living among them. It was a command. I knew where I had to go."[8]

WHAT REASONS DO CHRISTIANS GIVE FOR HUMAN DIGNITY?

Every person, from the first moment of his life in the womb, has an inviolable dignity, because from all eternity God willed, loved, created, and redeemed that person and destined him for eternal happiness.

If human dignity were based solely on the successes and accomplishments of individuals, then those who are weak, sick, or helpless would have no dignity. Christians believe that human dignity is, in the first place, the result of God's respect for us. He looks at every person and loves him as though he were the only creature in the world. Because God has looked upon even the least significant child of Adam, that person possesses an infinite worth, which must not be destroyed by men.

— YOUCAT, 280[10]

In that moment, and through her "yes" to its call, Sister Teresa of Loreto passed away and Mother Teresa of Calcutta was born. On April 12, 1948, she received permission to live outside her convent. She quickly set out for the slums of Calcutta where she first met the woman in the road, and eventually thousands of others who she helped serve, feed, and die with dignity. Her "call within a call" also led her to found the Missionaries of Charity, whose purpose was to care for "the hungry, the naked, the homeless, the crippled, the blind, the lepers, all those people who feel unwanted, unloved, and uncared for throughout society."

Over the next two decades, word spread about the nun's extraordinary work. In 1969, British reporter Malcolm Muggeridge profiled Mother Teresa in his acclaimed documentary, *Something Beautiful for God* (later a book by the same name). The film captivated the world as people fell in love with the steel-willed and golden-hearted saint. In 1979, she was awarded the Nobel Peace Prize. And in 1999, two years after her death, Americans voted her the "Most Admired Person of the Twentieth Century."[9]

Few saints have matched the global popularity Mother Teresa achieved during her lifetime. Although many claimed her as a saint even decades before her death in 1997, Pope John Paul II officially named her "Blessed Teresa of Calcutta" on October 19, 2003.

"YOU-DID-IT-TO-ME"

The Christian Church has a long history of saints who helped the poor, sick, and dying. And, like so many others, Mother Teresa devoted herself to this vital work. But what sets her apart is the way she not only served people in need, but dignified them. That's what makes her a model for the first major theme of Catholic social teaching, the life and dignity of the human person.

From the time of her birth in 1910, Agnes Bojaxhiu (Mother Teresa) was trained to respect the dignity of others, even those society ignores. Each weeknight Agnes' mother invited poor people into their home for dinner and conversation. She especially welcomed women in distress: old widows with no caretakers, homeless women with no roof, and unwed mothers shunned by family and friends. Agnes' brother later commented that, "[Our mother] never allowed any of the many poor people who came to our door to leave empty handed. When we would look at her strangely, she would say, 'Keep in mind that even those who are not our blood relatives, even if they are poor, are still our brethren.'"

It was through serving these visitors that Agnes first discovered "Jesus in his most distressing disguise." She came to value the poor not because of what they could do or produce, not because of their job or credentials, but because they radiated the image of God. According to the *Catechism of the Catholic Church*, "The dignity of the human person is rooted in his creation in the image and likeness of God" (CCC 1700). Thus, from the beginning until now, every man and woman bears the divine image and so bears within an inestimable dignity.

People often asked Mother Teresa why she loved the poor so much, how she could honor dignity in such difficult situations. In response, she liked to grasp their hand, slowly wiggle one finger at a time, and explain: "You-did-it-to-me." In her mind, you could count the whole Gospel on just five fingers.

She was alluding to Matthew 25 where Jesus teaches about the final judgment. Our Lord explains that at the end of the world he will judge people by their deeds of mercy. To the kind and giving, he will say, "Come you who are blessed by my Father.... For I was hungry and you gave me food, I was thirsty and you gave me drink, a stranger and you welcomed me, naked and you clothed me, ill and you cared for me, in prison and you visited me." But his surprised listeners ask, "Lord, when did we see you hungry and feed you, or thirsty and give you a drink?" Jesus replies, "Amen, I say to you, whatever you did for one of these least brothers of mine, you did for me."

For Mother Teresa, this passage wasn't just a pious metaphor. It described reality. The secret to her infectious joy and boundless compassion was that in every person — every paralytic, every leper, every invalid, and every orphan — she recognized Jesus.

DAILY PRAYER FOR MOTHER TERESA'S 'CHILDREN'S HOME'

Dearest Lord, may I see you today and every day in the person of your sick, and, whilst nursing them, ministering them unto you.

Though you hide yourself behind the unattractive disguise of the irritable, the exacting, the unreasonable, may I still recognize you, and say: "Jesus, my patient, how sweet it is to serve you."

Lord, give me this seeing faith, then my work will never be monotonous. I will ever find joy in humoring the fancies and gratifying the wishes of all poor sufferers.

O beloved sick, how doubly dear you are to me, when you personify Christ; and what a privilege is mine to be allowed to tend you.

Sweetest Lord, make me appreciative of the dignity of any high vocation, and its many responsibilities. Never permit me to disgrace it by giving way to coldness, unkindness, or impatience.

And O God, while you are Jesus, my patient, deign also to be to me a patient Jesus, bearing with my faults, looking only to my intention, which is to love and serve you in the person of each of your sick.

Lord, increase my faith, bless my efforts and work, now and for evermore. Amen.[11]

A Hindu gentleman once approached Mother Teresa and pointed out that while both he and Mother were doing social work, the difference was that he and his coworkers were doing it for *something* while Mother Teresa was doing it for *someone*. The compassionate nun didn't help people simply because "it was the right thing to do." She helped them because she knew, deep in her bones, that by serving others she was serving Jesus himself.

MOTHER TERESA'S SECRET

Learning to see Jesus among the poor, sick, and dying was no accident. Mother trained herself to do this each day. A young priest once prayed the Rosary with her, and when they finished, he spontaneously asked, "Mother Teresa, what is your secret?" She looked at him with a quizzical twinkle in her eye and replied, "That's very simple: I pray."[12]

Like all Christians, Mother Teresa found strength and sustenance through prayer. It brought her close to Christ and helped her know him in a personal way. But she valued her favorite form of prayer — the Liturgy — for another reason: it helped her recognize Christ in others.

Mother and her sisters celebrated Mass every morning at 4:30 a.m. For them, the liturgy, the Eucharist in particular, was key to living out Matthew 25 — to seeing Christ in the poor. In the Eucharist, Jesus becomes present under the form of ordinary bread and wine.

When the priest says the words of consecration, Christ becomes substantially present even if he's not evident to our senses. Our faith helps us transcend sensory experience to spot the divine image in its most ordinary form.

Mother Teresa knew how crucial this was. Seeing Christ in the Eucharist enabled her to see him in the streets. "If we recognize [Jesus] under the appearance of bread," she explained, "we will have no difficulty recognizing him in the disguise of the suffering poor."[13] This is why Mother Teresa could say, "I have an opportunity to be with Jesus 24 hours a day." Whether in the chapel or the slums, the pew or the hospital, she recognized the Lord everywhere she went because she trained herself each morning at the altar.

SMALL THINGS WITH GREAT LOVE

Another key to Mother Teresa's dignifying work was her focus on individuals. "If I look at the mass [of people],"she said, "I will never act. If I look at the one, I will." Along the same lines, she noted, "Jesus said love one another. He didn't say love the whole world."

One story illustrates this point. Some of her Sisters once discovered a man on a reservation in Australia, completely ignored by his fellow Aborigines. The man never left his house, and when the Sisters visited they found it extremely dirty and disordered.

Sometime later, Mother Teresa arrived. And when she did, she begged the man, "Please let me clean your house. Let me wash your clothes and make your bed."

The man declined. So the nun persisted: "You will be better if you allow me to do it."

Eventually, the man agreed. While Mother Teresa cleaned his house and washed his clothes, she discovered a beautiful lamp. It was covered with dust and looked as if it had not been lit for years.

"Don't you light that lamp?" she asked the man.

"Why would I?" he answered. "For whom? No one ever comes to my house. I spend days without ever seeing a human face. I have no need to light the lamp."

Mother Teresa replied, "Would you light it every night if my Sisters came?"

"Of course," the man said.

From that day on, the Sisters committed themselves to visiting him every day, and they did so without fail. Two years later, they received a letter from the lonely man, which he asked they pass on to Mother Teresa. It said, "Tell

ST. MARTIN'S CLOAK

Another saint who experienced the connection between serving others and serving Christ was St. Martin of Tours (316–397). On one cold winter day, the young Martin rode his horse through the gates of a wealthy town. He proudly displayed his sturdy armor, gleaming helmet, and a beautiful white cloak lined with lambswool. But then he spotted a poor beggar nearby. The man, whose clothes were ragged, stood shivering in the cold. Overcome with compassion, Martin took out his sword, slashed his cloak in two, and handed one half to the freezing man.

Many people laughed and jeered at Martin but later that night, as he slept, he dreamed that he saw Jesus wearing the half cloak he had given the beggar. Jesus gathered the angels and saints around him and said, "See! This is the cloak that Martin gave me."

From that day on, Martin knew what Mother Teresa knew: when we help the poor and marginalized, we help Jesus himself.

my friend that the light she lit in my life still continues to shine."[14]

To the casual observer, lighting a dusty lamp in a forgotten home might seem insignificant. What impact could that possibly have? What would that change? But that simple move meant the world to that one man. In his dark loneliness, Mother lit a light that continued to shine, and in doing so, she illumined his dignity.

We're often tempted to dismiss small acts of charity. But these acts have enormous potential. As Mother liked to say, "We ourselves feel that what we are doing is just a drop in the ocean. But if that drop was not in the ocean, I think the ocean will be less because of that missing drop."[15]

The great twentieth-century Doctor of the Church, St. Thérèse of Lisieux, after whom Mother Teresa took her name, taught that God doesn't always call us to do great things, but small things with great love. It's most often through small things, not big things, that we promote the dignity of others.

Mother once walked down a street in London and spotted a tall, thin man in the corner, huddled up and looking miserable. She walked over to him, smiled, shook his hand, and asked how he was.

He was stunned. He looked up at her and said, "Oh! After such a long, long, long time I feel the warmth of a human hand!" A smile slowly crept across his face.[16]

Mother later explained that "just shaking [that man's] hand made him feel like somebody." She always maintained that the easiest way to honor someone's dignity is through small acts: shaking someone's hand, flashing a smile, taking the time to listen. Though simple, these small gestures loudly proclaim, "You matter. You're important. You're worth my attention and affection."

THE GREATEST THREAT TO DIGNITY

Mother Teresa spent most of her energy serving the sick and dying in Calcutta. But when she traveled the world to speak, she often focused on another problem, one Pope Benedict XVI called "today's gravest injustice": abortion. On February 5, 1994, President Bill Clinton invited Mother to speak at the National Prayer Breakfast in Washington, D.C. She surprised many in attendance, including the President, when she used her talk to condemn the killing of unborn children:

"[Abortion] is a war against the child, a direct killing of the innocent child.... Many people are very, very concerned with the children of India, with the children of Africa where quite a few die of hunger, and so on. Many people are also concerned about all the violence in this great country of the United States. These concerns are very good. But often these same people are not concerned with the millions who are being killed by the deliberate decision of their own mothers. And this is the greatest destroyer of peace today — abortion which brings people to such blindness....

"But what does God say to us? He says: 'Even if a mother could forget her child, I will not forget you. I have carved you in the palm of my hand.' We are carved in the palm of His hand; that unborn child has been carved in the hand of God from conception and is called by God to love and to be loved, not only now in this life, but forever. God can never forget us."[17]

In her speech, Mother suggested countering the indignity of abortion through the dignifying act of adoption. While abortion says to a child, "We don't want you," adoption says to the child, "We do want you; you're valuable and needed." Mother noted how her children's home in Calcutta had saved over 3,000 children from abortion, children who were then adopted and given the chance to grow up full of love and joy.

To respect the dignity of all, we must respect it in the most vulnerable and defenseless among us. That includes the poor, the sick, and the dying, but it especially includes the unborn child. Every person carries the image of God, for, as Dr. Seuss put it, "A person's a person, no matter how small."[18]

LESSONS FROM BL. TERESA OF CALCUTTA

It's easy to disregard Mother Teresa by thinking, "I'll never be able to do what she did. I can't help thousands of forgotten street people," or, "I'll never serve someone dying of leprosy or hunger." Yet Mother's witness provides several ways that we can recognize and promote dignity in our ordinary, everyday lives.

First, we can cultivate our ability to see the image of God, to recognize and reverence the infinite value of each human life. The more we train the eyes of our hearts to spot Jesus in the Eucharist, the clearer we'll recognize him in the poor. During Mass, and throughout the day, pray the words of the blind beggar: "Lord, please let me see" (Lk 18:41). We can let that phrase bubble-up spontaneously whenever we're tempted to ignore or dismiss another person in need. Likewise, when we encounter someone in whom the divine image is clouded, we can remind ourselves that by helping this person we're helping Jesus — not in some vague, indirect way, but directly and literally. Remember: "You-did-it-to-me" (see Mt 25:40).

Second, we should look for ways to do small things with great love. Perhaps next time we encounter a homeless beggar, we can address his material needs, but also look into his eyes and smile. Mother maintained that "love begins with a smile." Even more, we can introduce ourselves. Ask his name, shake his hand, promise to pray for him and then actually do it. (It's best to say a silent prayer immediately after you meet, before you forget.) In one of her disconcerting aphorisms, Mother noted, "Today it is very fashionable to talk about the poor. Unfortunately it is very unfashionable to talk with them."[19]

Finally, we must focus on individuals. Mother once said:

> "I never look at the masses as my responsibility; I look at the individual. I can only love one person at a time — just one, one, one. So you begin. I began — I picked up one person. Maybe if I didn't pick up that one person, I wouldn't have picked up forty-two thousand.... The same thing goes for you, the same thing in your family, the same thing in your church, your community. Just begin — one, one, one."

We don't need to travel to India to honor dignity like Mother Teresa. We can do so right in your own homes and workplaces, with our family, friends, and coworkers. In fact, Mother was fond of telling visitors to go home and find their own Calcutta. In every city, countless individuals suffer the cruel fate of loneliness and indignity. The elderly woman living three houses down from us whom nobody checks on. The janitor who washes the halls each day, never receiving eye contact. The forgotten man living out his last months in the nursing home. All of these people cry out through silent urges: "Notice me! Consider me! Help me!" We may not be able to serve the poor in a third-world country but we can honor the dignity of those who live and work around us.

Mother Teresa helps us see that it's not our job to help millions at a time. We can only help individuals, and we do that first by recognizing and reverencing the image of God marked on their souls, and by serving Jesus in them through small acts of dignifying love.

CHAPTER 2
ST. PETER CLAVER

I've always been attracted to saints who accomplish magnificent feats with little to no fanfare. Sure, you've got St. Paul evangelizing the whole known world, then you have St. Ignatius launching a global religious order, and then there's St. Padre Pio working miracles left and right. But I also admire saints like Peter Claver, who might not be well-known today, but who profoundly affected the Church and the world.

Peter was born on June 25, 1580, in Catalonia, Spain. From a young age, his poor but deeply Catholic parents modeled for him humility and obedience, emphasizing that the least actions done for God are great in his sight.

Their example greatly inspired Peter. While studying at a Jesuit-run university in Barcelona, he recorded these words in his notebook: "I must dedicate myself to the service of God until death, on the understanding that I am like a slave." Little did he know how prophetic his words would become.

At the age of 20, after acquiring multiple degrees at the university, Peter decided to become a Jesuit. He entered the Society of Jesus in 1602. Then, after three years of study in the novitiate, Peter was sent to Majorca to study philosophy and divinity.

It was there he met a man who would change his life forever. Alphonsus Rodriguez was the porter at Majorca, a simple but holy man. He guarded the door, ran errands, and distributed alms. Yet he was poorly educated and had difficulty meeting the Jesuits' rigorous academic requirements.

However, what Alphonsus lacked in intellect, he made up for in piety. People flocked to the door-keeper for spiritual guidance and for his special gift of prophecy. As the local provincial said, "If Alphonsus wasn't qualified to become a brother or a priest [in the Jesuits], he could enter to become a saint."[20]

Like most others, Peter Claver gravitated toward the holy porter. Alphonsus taught many of the same virtues as his parents, such as obedience and charity. One day, as Peter approached his friend, Alphonsus surprised him with a prophecy: God wanted Peter to journey to the Spanish territories in North America, where he would serve and save many souls. Peter was surprised, but intrigued. He had always wanted to be a missionary and was excited by the idea of evangelizing the New World. So he decided to go.

In April 1610, Peter set sail for the missions. After many long difficult months of travel, he arrived at Cartagena, in what is now Colombia. He would never see his homeland again.

THE SUPREME VILLAINY

If the sixteenth century was defined by religious and scientific revolution, the seventeenth century was a time of expansion. New lands meant new needs, as the settlers in Central and South America required laborers to cultivate their newly conquered soil. They also needed able bodies to work their gold and silver mines. They first turned to the local Indians, many of whom they captured and enslaved. They forced the Indians to work in grueling conditions in the mines, but soon realized they were generally not physically suited for that sort of work.

So they turned to Africa instead. The African slave trade had been gaining steam, as monarchs, like the emperor Charles V, promoted and profited from it. New settlers in the Americas followed suit and sought slave labor from the West African coasts of Guinea, the Congo, and Angola.

West African dealers either captured the slaves or bought them for around four crowns a head. They then sold each slave for an average of two hundred crowns. That enormous profit meant that most dealers were unconcerned with the health of any particular slave. Even if many died from sickness or hunger during trip to the New World, they would still remain profitable. To them, slaves were disposable objects and keys to profit, not human beings with dignity.

The journey across the Atlantic Ocean took several months, and the conditions aboard the slave ships were indescribably foul and inhuman. The slaves spent all day and night chained to one another, with little food or water. Human waste smeared the floor and disease was rampant. It's estimated that during each trip, one-third of the slaves died in transit.

By the time Peter landed at Cartagena for his missionary work, the prosperous port-city had become the chief slave-mart of the New World. Ten thousand new slaves poured in each year, mostly from West Africa. The Catholic locals welcomed the cheap labor even as their Church publicly denounced it. Popes Paul III and Urban VIII vigorously condemned slavery — Pope Urban calling it a "supreme villainy" — but the lucrative business continued to flourish.

This left the local priests feeling powerless. As boat after boat arrived, they pleaded and protested for more humane conditions. In response, all most slave-owners did was to have their slaves baptized. Yet since the slaves had little religious formation regarding the sacrament, they soon associated baptism with oppression. For them baptism was just one more mark of bondage, a branding with cool water instead of hot iron.

Peter witnessed all of this during his first years in Cartagena. He realized how large and powerful the slave trade was, and he wondered what he could possibly do to stop it. He sensed that while he couldn't suppress this great injustice, he could at least alleviate the sufferring by promoting the dignity of the slaves.

IT'S GOOD THAT YOU EXIST

Before he became Pope Francis, Cardinal Jorge Bergoglio faced many problems as Archbishop of Buenos Aires, Argentina. High poverty rates, massive drug addiction, and powerful gangs all concerned him, but one problem seemed to root all the other issues. He noted in a 2013 interview:

"The biggest problem we face is marginalization of the people. Drugs are a symptom, violence is a symptom, but marginalization is the disease. Our people feel marginalized by a social system that's forgotten about them and isn't interested in them.... Marginalization is the mother of our problems, and unfortunately she has many children.... Basically, what society is telling these people is, 'We don't want you to exist.' The work we're doing here is to try to tell them instead, 'It's good that you exist.'"[21]

That response — "It's good that you exist" — carries great power. To someone struggling with alcohol, who drinks away his loneliness, we say, "It's good that you exist." To someone who loathes her body and thinks she's too fat, too skinny, too short, or not good enough, we say, "It's good that you exist." To the addict, the slave, the homeless man, even the murderer, we say, "It's good that you exist."

This phrase reminds people that they have intrinsic value, regardless of what they produce, or how they look, or if they have it all together. It echoes what God said immediately after creating the first man: "[He] looked at everything he had made, and found it very good" (Gn 1:31).

Next time you want to uplift someone's dignity, remind them of that wonderful truth: "It's good that you exist."

'SLAVE OF THE SLAVES'

On March 19, 1616, Peter Claver was ordained a priest in Cartagena — the first Jesuit ordained in the city. He immediately set out for the work that would consume the rest of his life: serving the African slaves.

His first move was to connect with Father Alfonso de Sandoval, a fellow Jesuit known for his ministry to slaves (not to be confused with Alphonsus the door-keeper). By the time Peter arrived, Alfonso had already been serving in Cartagena for over 40 years. He took Peter under his wing and taught him many lessons. For example, Alfonso shared how valuable it was to learn the African customs and languages, for if you spoke in words and symbols that the slaves recognized, you would quickly gain their trust.

Working with Father Alfonso solidified Peter's mission to the slaves. As he witnessed their degrading conditions, and the ways their dignity was trampled over, he knew he wanted to devote his life to them. He began identifying himself as "Petrus Claver, Aethiopum servus" — Peter Claver, slave of the Africans. (He would later become known more generally as the "Slave of the Slaves.")

Alfonso and Peter served the same people but in different ways. Alfonso visited the slaves where they worked, usually in the mines or plantations. But Peter chose to meet them on the slave ships as soon as they arrived. He wanted their first experience of the New World to be one of compassion and dignity.

Each month when the slave ships appeared, Peter sailed out to them on a small boat. He climbed aboard and met slaves on the deck. Then he hurried

EXCERPT FROM ST. PETER CLAVER LETTER

"Yesterday, May 30, 1627, on the feast of the Most Holy Trinity, numerous blacks, brought from the rivers of Africa, disembarked from a large ship. Carrying two baskets of oranges, lemons, sweet biscuits, and I know not what else, we hurried toward them.... We had to force our way through the crowd until we reached the sick. Large numbers of the sick were lying on wet ground or rather in puddles of mud ... they were naked, without any clothing to protect them....

"Then, using our own cloaks ... we [covered them].... The joy in their eyes as they looked at us was something to see.

"[W]e spoke to them, not with words but with our hands and our actions. And in fact, convinced as they were that they had been brought here to be eaten, any other language would have proved utterly useless. Then we sat, or rather knelt, beside them and bathed their faces and bodies with wine. We made every effort to encourage them with friendly gestures and displayed in their presence the emotions which somehow naturally tend to hearten the sick."[22]

down to the filthy and putrid holds, the floors covered with mud and feces, and offered whatever poor refreshments he could afford. He found it difficult to move around since the slaves were shackled close together. But as Peter navigated the crowd, he smiled and greeted each person, passing out fruits, biscuits, sweets, and tobacco. You can imagine the impact this had. Most slaves were sick and terrified and hadn't seen a friendly face for months. Few had ever received such generosity.

Peter's kindness offered a breath of fresh air in an otherwise hellish inferno. It showed the slaves that this man was no oppressor: he was their defender and friend, one who believed they deserved the same respect as all other people.

SAVING SOULS AND DIGNIFYING SLAVES

Many of the local clergy, including several of Peter's Jesuit brothers, decided that since they didn't speak any of the African languages, they were exempt from helping the slaves. But Peter didn't buy that excuse. He taught himself the language of Angola, since many of the slaves came from there, and hired teams of interpreters to help with other languages. Following Alfonso's advice, he also carried to the slaves large pictures with basic instructions about the faith. His main goal was to restore their self-respect by explaining how they were made in the image of God and thus had dignity and worth. You are loved, he would tell them, and nothing can take that away.

It was an uphill battle. Besides the language barriers, the slaves were bitter and suspicious of Peter's charity. Yet, through persistence and patience, he overcame their resistances. Peter baptized over 300,000 African slaves during his ministry, more baptisms than any saint in Church history (though depending on which account you read, his fellow Jesuit St. Francis Xavier may have bested him). To transcend the language problems, he creatively chose to baptize slaves in groups of ten, giving them all the same name so it would be easier for them to remember.

These baptisms saved their souls, of course. But they were important for other reasons, too. First, they indelibly marked each slave as a child of God. They expressed to the slaves that they were not merely property, bartering objects, or cheap sources of labor. They were invaluable sons and daughters of God, deeply loved and divinely dignified.

Baptism also made a public statement. It lifted the slaves onto an equal plane with their masters. Some locals criticized Peter for "profaning" the sacrament by baptizing creatures whom they believed scarcely possessed a soul. Others complained that inviting slaves into a church desecrated it. Peter responded by quoting from St. Paul, who taught there is "one Lord, one faith, [and] one baptism" (Eph 4:5). He baptized slaves into the same waters, with the same formula, and into the same Church as their owners and masters, thereby communicating that whether black or white, rich or poor, slave or free, all emerged from the baptismal waters as members of the same Body of the Christ.

> ## IMPRINTED WITH GOD'S IMAGE
>
> "Human persons are willed by God; they are imprinted with God's image. Their dignity does not come from the work they do, but from the persons they are."
>
> — St. John Paul II[23]

HOSPITALS, PLANTATIONS, AND PRISONS

Peter didn't only serve slaves while they were on the ship. He stayed in touch with them long after they were sold. Unlike English slavery in the Caribbean, Spanish law allowed slaves to marry and forbade the splitting up of families. Peter made sure owners respected this law. He sporadically visited the towns around Cartagena to check on his slave friends. When the owners offered Peter lavish rooms on their plantations, he chose to stay in the slave quarters, causing no small tension.

Peter also regularly heard the slaves' confessions. This grated against the Spanish nobility, who appealed to Peter's superior to mandate that Peter hear their confessions first (they were aware of Peter's saintly reputation and fame). Yet Peter would make them wait until he had seen all the slaves, responding: "I am not the proper confessor for fine ladies. You should go to some other confessor. My confessional was never meant for ladies of quality. It is too narrow for their gowns. It is only suited to poor Negresses."[24]

Peter was said to have heard the confessions of more than five thousand slaves per year. At times, he sat in the hot confessional so long that he fainted, and had to be awakened with vinegar.

Besides meeting spiritual needs, each week Peter also visited the two hospitals in Cartagena, St. Sebastian and St. Lazarus, the latter specifically built for lepers. Even though leprosy was contagious, Peter served the patient's spiritual and physical needs. Noting the squalid conditions, he later joked that, "If being a saint consists in having no taste and a strong stomach, I admit I may be one."[25]

Peter also spent much time in the prisons, especially with those awaiting execution. He listened to their stories, consoled them, and affirmed that even though their bodies were behind bars they were truly free children of God.

The difficult conditions took a toll on his body. In 1650, at seventy years old, Peter contracted a virulent plague that spread through Cartagena. The illness wore him down rapidly. Though it didn't kill him, it left him in constant pain. It also produced an uncontrollable tremor that kept him from celebrating Mass. He spent his last days isolated in a cell with few visitors. Religious authorities paid little attention to Peter until one day, though feeble and inactive, he was falsely accused of rebaptizing Africans. The religious leaders banned Peter from ever baptizing again in the future, a cruel and humiliating fate for someone who had baptized thousands.

Peter never complained in the face of persecution. Channeling the humility he learned from his parents and mentors, he compared himself to a donkey: "When he is evilly spoken of he is dumb. When he is starved he is dumb. When he is overloaded he is dumb. When he is despised and neglected he is still dumb. He never complains in any circumstances for he is only a donkey. So also must God's servant be."[26]

Peter hung on for several more years, until 1654, when he was joined by Fr. Diego Ramirez Farina, a Spanish missionary who aimed to continue Peter's work. Fr. Diego's presence overjoyed Peter, and gave him great relief that his ministry to the slaves would continue. Within days of Fr. Diego's arrival, Peter lapsed into a coma and died.

Though mocked and belittled by local authorities during his lifetime, Peter was immediately recognized as a national hero upon his death. Civil and religious leaders scrambled over each other to honor his memory, burying Peter with impressive ceremony and at great expense. The Africans and Indians arranged their own special Mass to celebrate their friend and protector, the "Slave of the Slaves." When they first heard of Peter's death, they visited his cell and stripped away everything to serve as relics of the saint, so great was their love for him.

In 1888, Pope Leo XIII officially canonized Peter Claver, along with his mentor Alphonsus Rodriguez, and declared him the patron of missionary work among the African people.

WELL, YOU HAVE ONE NOW

As a high school senior in the 1960s, Victor was like any other boy. He loved to dance and play sports and was beloved by his classmates. But then he contracted leprosy, now known as Hansen's disease. Doctors immediately sent him away to a leprosarium in Carville, Louisiana. During his six lonely years there, doctors discovered drugs that could halt the disease's effects. But not before it had ravaged Victor's body. The disease left him blind in one eye, with a limp, and with only partial use of his hands. Worse, it badly disfigured his face such that people could hardly look at him.

By the time Victor returned home, his old friends abandoned him, and even his parents could not bear his deformities. He began living on the streets where he was afraid to show himself in daylight. He sank into depression, a man with nowhere to turn and nobody who cared.

But then he remembered a kind priest who had once shown him compassion. Bishop Fulton Sheen, a well-known television preacher, had visited Victor and other patients at the leprosarium. Victor never forgot how Sheen treated them with dignity and respect. Even though he wasn't Catholic, Victor decided to write the Bishop and ask for an appointment.

To his surprise, Bishop Sheen responded. He invited Victor to his office in New York. When Victor arrived, he sat down and cut right to the chase, explaining: "I've come to you because I have no one to turn to. I haven't a friend in the world."

Sheen responded immediately: "Well, you have one now."

Sheen honored that promise in the following years by supporting Victor in many ways. He helped him into an apartment. He gave him food and clothes. He even set Victor up with a behind-the-scenes job where his disfigurement would not be an impediment.

Most impressively, Bishop Sheen invited Victor over for dinner to his home once a week. Since Victor had difficulty using his hands, the Bishop personally cut his food for him during each meal. He treated Victor as a member of his own family and, thanks to this dignifying love, Victor eventually regained his confidence. He not only began showing himself in public, but proudly sat in the front row of the cathedral as Bishop Sheen was installed Bishop of Rochester in 1966.[27]

Though Sheen gave Victor money, medicine, and material help, his greatest gift was attentive friendship, a friendship not based on looks or utility but on love.

LESSONS FROM ST. PETER CLAVER

When looking to Peter Claver as an example of promoting the life and dignity of every person, we find several practical lessons. First, Peter models the urgency with which we must confront the tragedy of slavery. Many people in Peter's day turned a blind eye to the practice by ignoring or denying it. And unfortunately, the same thing occurs today. Most people are unaware that according to the United Nations, 27 million people are trapped in slavery right now — more than at any point in human history.[28] That number includes an estimated 40,000 slaves on U.S. soil, most of whom are women and children, the victims of human trafficking.[29]

This tragedy is of course too big for any one person to defeat — even someone as magnanimous as Peter Claver. But we can each do our small part. A good first step is to become familiar with the U.S. Conference of Catholic Bishops' Anti-Trafficking Program.[30] The Bishops' renowned program has achieved great success in rescuing human trafficking victims and helping them regain their sense of dignity. Its website contains plenty of information on how to identify victims in our local community and help become part of the solution.

Beyond that, consider attending to other less evident, but just as serious forms of slavery. Alcohol and drug addiction, for example, are forms of bondage that trap millions of people each year. Pornography enslaves millions of viewers and reduces men and women to sexual objects, thereby stripping them of their God-given dignity. We must help all people trapped in bondage to rediscover their value and freedom, following Jesus' own declaration: "The

Spirit of the Lord … has sent me to proclaim liberty to captives and … to let the oppressed go free" (Lk 4:18).

A second lesson we can learn from Peter Claver is not to submit to excuses. Many of Peter's Jesuit brothers refused to serve the slaves, and they came up with many reasons why: they didn't speak the African languages, the slave trade was too established and difficult to change, and serving the slaves meant risking their own health. But Peter didn't let those worries block his charitable service. We must not either. If Martin Luther King Jr. was right that, "injustice anywhere is a threat to justice everywhere," then every attack on dignity, from the moment of conception until natural death, is an attack worth confronting. Fear and timidity should never discourage our charity.

Finally, the primary way Peter helped slaves recognize their own value was by teaching them how much God loved them. That simple truth may seem trite today — "Jesus loves me, this I know …" — but it still has life-changing power. The most remarkable fact that anyone can know is that God uniquely created you in love, and he desires you, cares for you, and values you immensely. Even more, this love has nothing to do with what you do or who you are. God's love is unearned and unconditional, a fact that gave hope to slaves four-hundred years ago and continues to dignify lives today.

CALL TO FAMILY, COMMUNITY, AND PARTICIPATION

The person is not only sacred but also social. How we organize our society — in economics and politics, in law and policy — directly affects human dignity and the capacity of individuals to grow in community. **Marriage and the family are the central social institutions that must be supported and strengthened, not undermined.** We believe people have a right and a duty to participate in society, seeking together the common good and well-being of all, especially the poor and vulnerable.[31]

CHAPTER 3

ST. FRANCES
OF ROME

I chose to write about St. Frances before I knew all the tragic details of her family life. But the more I learned about her faith and fortitude, the more I became inspired as a father and husband. As you read her story, you will be touched and saddened by the losses she endured, but I encourage you to look beyond the waves of trouble and appreciate the wisdom and grace she applied to both family and community life.

The Church faced serious problems when Frances Bussa was born in 1384. The papacy had fallen under the influence of the French Crown and had developed a reputation for corruption. Worse, in 1378 a majority of bishops elected a new pope, Robert of Geneva, even though a legitimate pope already reigned, which launched the Great Schism of the West. The abuses, confusion, and conflict fractured the Church, causing internal strain and civil wars. Frances' whole life would play out during the forty years of the schism.

Thankfully, the young girl's parents shielded her from the schism's worst effects. Paul and Jacobella each belonged to illustrious and wealthy families in Rome. Jacobella was quiet and pious, while townspeople revered Paul for his firm leadership and resolve. Both were deeply religious. When Frances was growing up, her family often visited Santa Maria Nuova, a nearby church served by Benedictine monks. They grew especially close to one monk, Dom Antonio. He became Jacobella's spiritual director, and she eventually entrusted Frances to Dom Antonio, too.

Frances was a notably pious girl. Feeling drawn to a life of solitude and prayer, she decided that God wanted her to become a nun. She never mentioned this to her parents, though she did tell Dom Antonio. The wise monk drew up a rule of life for the girl, a way to test-drive the ascetic demands of religious life before permanently committing to them.

Frances loved the lifestyle. It was everything she hoped for. She spent hours alone in prayer, conversing with God, and engaged in tough sacrifices to strengthen her will. At the age of eleven, she made up her mind. She wanted to become a nun. She went to her parents to ask their permission to enter the convent.

Her mother was initially open to the idea. She noted how Frances seemed inclined to the religious life. However, her father adamantly refused. If that wasn't startling enough for young Frances, he explained that the reason he refused was because he had already arranged for her to marry Lorenzo Ponziano, a young boy from a noble family. As a man of his word, nothing would convince her father to renege on the promise.

Frances raced off in tears. She pleaded with God to prevent the marriage and ran to Dom Antonio, begging him to help change her father's mind. After listening to her laments, Dom Antonio replied: "Are you crying because you want to do God's will or because you want God to do your will?"[32]

The question slowed Frances' tears. She knew she wanted to be a nun, but she wasn't sure if that's what God had in mind. Though still troubled, she returned home and announced that she would obey her father's decision. She still yearned to enter a religious community, but by marrying Lorenzo she would find community in a different way.

FINDING GOD THROUGH FAMILY

At first glance, the marriage looked ideal. Other young women would have been overjoyed to marry a man like Lorenzo. He was handsome, noble, wealthy, and had a good heart. As commander of Rome's papal troops, he was greatly esteemed and lived lavishly.

But for the shy Frances, this was a nightmare. Her mother-in-law, Cecilia, pushed her hard, grooming her to be an active and outgoing hostess. After an elaborate wedding and a whirl of parties and banquets, the thirteen-year-old girl collapsed due to exhaustion. Frances lay close to death for months, unable to eat or speak, and even prayed for God to take her life.

Yet one day she had a vision of St. Alexis, a fifth-century boy who, like her, was forced into an unwanted marriage. In the vision, Alexis told Frances that God was offering her a similar choice: she could either recover or not. She could become a devoted bride or give up and flee this life. The decision was hers and God would grant whatever she chose.

Though completely miserable, Frances' devotion trumped her weakness. She whispered, "God's will is mine." St. Alexis replied, "Then you will live to glorify His Name." Upon hearing that answer, Frances sat up, immediately healed of her fatigue, and set out to serve her husband. This new resolve didn't mean her problems went away. Francis still felt inadequate as a wife. Frances and Lorenzo lived in a sprawling palace along with Frances' mother-in-law, Cecilia; Lorenzo's brother, Paluzzo; Paluzzo's wife, Vanozza; and several servants. Cecilia constantly chided Frances for not being as bubbly and outgoing as Vanozza, who delighted in elegant parties, fancy dress, and was a very devoted wife.

The complaints stung Frances and many times brought her to tears. One day, Vanozza discovered Frances sobbing in the garden. When she asked what was wrong, Frances poured her heart out. She revealed her struggles, her sickness, and her vision of St. Alexis. She complained that her life of frivolous recreation prevented her from pursuing her true desire, which was to dedicate herself to the Lord.

When Frances finished venting, Vanozza bent down, comforted the young girl, and revealed that she too preferred to give herself wholly to God, and that married life was not easy for her, either. Yet once she learned to see marriage as an outlet for her dedication to God, not as a competitor with it, things completely changed.

CREATED FOR COMMUNITY

"But God did not create man as a solitary, for from the beginning 'male and female he created them' (Gen. 1:27). Their companionship produces the primary form of interpersonal communion. For by his innermost nature man is a social being, and unless he relates himself to others he can neither live nor develop his potential."

— *Gaudium et Spes*, 12

Frances was revived by discovering a kindred spirit within the family. She and Vanozza decided to help each other flourish in their vocation as wives. They created a mutual plan for holiness: they would live their married duties with deep commitment, serve their husbands as if serving the Lord, and maintain their interior sanctuary through prayer, almsgiving, and penance.

They visited local hospitals together to help nurse the sick and distribute food and clothing. Frances kept up weekly confession with Dom Antonio and weekly communion. At home, the two sisters-in-law created a secret oratory in an old building where they would pray quietly once their duties were complete.

Vanozza helped Frances see that becoming a wife didn't mean leaving God behind. It meant finding God even more deeply through the ordinary duties of marriage. As Frances later affirmed in the quote she's most remembered for: "A married woman must, when called upon, quit her devotions to God at the altar, to find him in her household affairs."[33]

In 1400, Frances gave birth to a son, Battista, the first of four children. A year later, Cecilia passed away and everyone in the Ponziano estate agreed that Frances should become mistress, despite her reticence and even though she was just sixteen years old. It turned out to be an excellent decision. Frances was an efficient administrator and a fair and charitable employer. She especially took notice of the servants' spiritual needs and they all came to love her.

FAMILY STRUGGLES AND TRAGEDY

Things continued to flourish over the years. Frances' second son, Evangelista, was born in 1404, and three years later she gave birth to her daughter, Agnes.

But then in 1408, civil war erupted in Rome. The conflict stemmed over rival claims to the papacy. Ladislaus, a ruthless commander who supported the antipope, sent a cruel governor, Count Troja, to conquer Rome.

The true Pope's supporters revolted against Troja making the city a battleground. Frances' husband, Lorenzo, played a key role in the fight but was stabbed during one of its many skirmishes. Troops carried him back to Frances, who began nursing him back to health.

The war brought even more pain to Frances and her family. After wreaking havoc on the true Pope's supporters, Troja decided to arrest their leaders. He rounded up Paluzzo, Frances' brother-in-law, and sought Lorenzo as well. But since Lorenzo was near death, he instead demanded their son, Battista, as a hostage. Troja knew that as long as he had Battista, the Ponzianos would not return to battle.

Frances was terrified. She grabbed Battista by the hand and ran to Dom Antonio, asking what to do. Surprisingly, the monk counseled her to comply, explaining that God would take care of the boy and that she just needed to trust him. Frances walked her son to Capitol Hill, where Troja waited with his troops. She turned over the boy and immediately fled to the nearest church, prostrating herself before a statue of the Virgin.

As soon as she left, Troja ordered his soldiers to lift Battista onto a horse. However, when the officer mounted the horse with the boy, the horse refused to move. The officer changed horses with the same result. They whipped the horses, yelled, and pushed them, but none would budge. The soldiers took this as a divine sign, and they sent the boy back. Frances was still lying down in prayer when she felt Battista's arm lifting her up.

Despite that momentary grace, more problems lay ahead. After Lorenzo recovered, the family sent him out of Rome to avoid capture, and that left the Ponziano estate vulnerable. One day, drunken vandals broke into the mansion and tore it apart, smashing everything in sight. They tortured and killed the servants, and they kidnapped Battista and carried him to Naples. As Frances sorted through the wreckage over the following weeks, the plague hit Rome, taking the life of her nine-year-old son, Evangelista. Then a year later, it took her daughter, Agnes.

We would hardly blame Frances for despairing after these Job-like tragedies. Her husband was gone, one son and one daughter dead, her other son hostage, and her house destroyed. Yet, instead, these hardships sensitized Frances to the needs of others who suffered. She decided to clear out the rubble and convert part of the estate into a makeshift hospital and homeless shelter. Along with her sister-in-law, Vanozza, she distributed food and wine reserves to anyone in need. She even sold the fancy jewels and clothes left over in the house, giving the money away.

Finally, in 1414, the political tension simmered. Each of the papal claimants resigned, and the Council of Constance elected Pope Martin V, essentially ending the schism. Lorenzo returned home, carrying the rescued Battista with him, and Frances directed all her energies back toward her family.

THE ORIGINAL CELL OF SOCIAL LIFE

"The family is the *original cell of social life*. It is the natural society in which husband and wife are called to give themselves in love and in the gift of life. Authority, stability, and a life of relationships within the family constitute the foundations for freedom, security, and fraternity within society. The family is the community in which, from childhood, one can learn moral values, begin to honor God, and make good use of freedom. Family life is an initiation into life in society."

— *Catechism of the Catholic Church*, 2207

NEW SPIRITUAL HOUSE

At this stage in his life, after suffering many battle wounds, Lorenzo could hardly do anything himself. He became completely dependent on Frances. In early 1425, he called his wife to him and announced that he wanted to release her from her marital duties. She could be free to pursue her contemplative longings. His only request was that she continue living at the estate.

Frances was thrilled. For years she had attracted a following of young, noble women — girls who admired Frances' commitment to family and charity. Frances had long wanted to form this group into a community where the women would carry out the works of mercy in their ordinary lives, while living under the Rule of St. Benedict. She brought her plan to Dom Antonio for review, and after his approval, on August 15, 1425, she officially launched the Oblates of Mary.

Strictly speaking, the group was not a religious order. They did not take vows, and initially lived in their own homes. Also, Frances never considered herself a religious founder. She remained occupied with nursing Lorenzo, so with her blessing, the community chose Agnes de Lellis as its first superior.

In 1432, Frances acquired an old building and converted it into a monastery. She then invited some of the members, mostly widows, to live together in community:

"My dear companions.... For seven years we have been especially consecrated ... to live in chastity and obedience, and to observe the rules prescribed to us.... But at last the Lord has revealed to me his will that I should found a new spiritual building in this city, the ancient stronghold of faith. It will form an asylum for women of your rank who have generously resolved to forsake all worldly allurements.... You are the foundations of the building, the first stones of the new spiritual house of Mary, his Mother. You are the seed from which a plentiful harvest is to spring."[34]

Even after establishing the monastery, Frances remained devoted to Lorenzo, choosing to stay home and take care of him. He finally passed away in 1436, and he used his final breaths to praise his devoted wife: "I feel as if my whole life has been one beautiful dream of purest happiness. God has given me so much in your love."[35]

On the feast of St. Benedict, Frances walked barefoot to the monastery she had founded. She lay prostrate on the ground, and begged the community to admit her. They of course agreed. Then, despite Frances' protests, Agnes de Lellis insisted on resigning, allowing the community to choose Frances as their new superior.

The next four years in the monastery were sheer bliss. Frances could spend all day moving from charity to contemplation to counseling the other sisters. She had mystical experiences in prayer and performed several miracles. It is said that during the last years of her life, she had direct vision of her guardian angel who aided her in service. On the evening of March 9, 1440, Frances' face glowed as she spoke her final words: "The angel has finished his work. He is beckoning me to follow."[36]

THE FIRST SCHOOL OF CHRISTIAN LIFE

Behind almost every saint is a holy family, and that was especially true for St. Thérèse of Lisieux. The young saint's father, Louis, trained her in prayer from a young age, often taking her to a nearby trout stream for lessons on contemplation and humility. Her mother, Zélie, taught Thérèse the value of small acts done with great love, and of serving those you live with even when they seem irritable. These lessons helped create an environment that became, for Thérèse, "the first school of Christian life" (CCC, 1657).

On October 19, 2008, as a testament to their venerable lives and parenting, Pope Benedict XVI beatified both Zélie and Louis. Yet they were not declared "blessed" because of Thérèse. She became a saint because of them. And that should be the aim of all parents and Christian families: to produce saints.

LESSONS FROM ST. FRANCES OF ROME

It took several decades to play out, but the eleven-year-old Frances was right in discerning her vocation. She *was* called to religious community — she just had the timing wrong. God had other plans before leading her to the Oblates of Mary including a sojourn in a different type of community: a family. Frances' life, both in the palace and the monastery, offers many lessons to us today.

First, holiness begins with the family. According to St. John Paul II, "as the family goes, so goes the nation and so goes the whole world."[37] Catholic social teaching considers the family the basic building block of society and the first school of community. All of us, especially those raising families, can pursue the same gifts as those in monasteries, without ever leaving our homes — deep prayer, almsgiving, chastity, and communion. Frances' early life shows that our spouses, children, and parents provide daily opportunities to live communally and to serve the Lord through serving others.

Second, Frances' life highlights the value of spiritual friendship. Without the help and support of her sister-in-law, Vanozza, Frances may have given up the pursuit of holiness. Yet Vanozza helped Frances see how to devote herself to God as a wife and mother. She provided a model for Frances to imitate, and encouragement during times of trouble.

It's often difficult to find good, spiritual friends to help us on the path to holiness — friends to pray with, think with, serve with. Yet as Vanozza shows, such friends may be nearer than we think. We should ask God to help us find spiritual companions, especially if they're people we're already close with. We can try opening up to others, making ourselves vulnerable, and sharing our spiritual hopes and desires. We may be surprised at their reactions. They may respond by uttering what William Barclay called the two most powerful words in the English language: "Me, too." And that reaction is fertile ground for deep and holy friendships.

Third, Frances shows that we can find community anywhere. Growing up, she assumed it was primarily found in monasteries. But over the first fifty years of her life, she discovered community in many other places. She found it in a dysfunctional estate, riddled with in-fighting; a post-war rebuilding effort, where food and comfort were rare; and finally alongside rich young women who sought holiness in their homes. Her experiences confirm that God wants us to commune with others wherever we happen to be, whether cities or suburbs, cubicles or farms, parishes or restaurants.

Finally, we should imitate Frances' fidelity. In our time when commitment is totteringly low, she provides a great example of faithfulness. She committed to Lorenzo and stuck with him until the end, despite her passions pulling her away and Lorenzo's poor health demanding attention. She committed to the women in her religious community, never wavering in her support and involvement. Finally, she committed to the Lord, unreservedly, trusting his path even when it seemed to veer far from what she had in mind. All community depends on people committing themselves to the good of others. Frances showed this throughout her life and gives us an important model.

CHAPTER 4
BL. ANNE MARIE
JAVOUHEY

History doesn't reveal many politically active saints. Most carried out their public duties in simple, ordinary ways, usually in isolation or through religious communities. But among the models we do have, Bl. Anne Marie Javouhey stands out for her creative public service. Imagine a cross between Mother Teresa and Dorothy Day, living in France during the rule of Napoleon, and you'll have a good picture of Anne Marie. Friends and family described her as a "velvet brick," a thin layer of gentleness covering a determined, compassionate core.

The fifth of nine children, Anne Marie was born in 1779, shortly before the French Revolution. She was raised by well-to-do farmers, who passed on an activist spirit that manifested itself at a young age. At around eight years old, the vivacious girl organized her brothers and sisters under a sort of junior religious congregation, complete with a self-designed Rule. The program included long periods of silence and recitation of the Liturgy of the Hours.

Yet the joys of family life were tinged by many difficulties. Throughout her early years, Anne Marie experienced the effects of political turmoil. The French Revolution raged on and the population became deeply hostile toward Catholicism. For example, in 1792, anticlerical revolutionaries set fire to a local chapel. Anne Marie rushed to the scene to rescue the worshipers and help clear the rubble. Afterward, friends often found her standing guard outside a church, looking for roving spies. Her family hid priests at home, and when angry mobs approached, Anne Marie misdirected them away.

This religious oppression forced Anne Marie, at an early age, to apply her organizing skills. As a teenager, she accompanied her father on trips into town where she passed and received information about priests-in-hiding. She arranged secret meet-ups in old barns where people could hear sermons at night, confess their sins, and attend sunrise Mass. As the Revolution took its toll across France, Anne Marie visited poor families to bring them bread and money. She taught catechism lessons to young children and prepared them for First Communion, which they received secretly in her father's barns.

THE OBLIGATION TO PARTICIPATE

"It is necessary that all participate, each according to his position and role, in promoting the common good. This obligation is inherent in the dignity of the human person.... As far as possible citizens should take an active part in public life."

— *Catechism of the Catholic Church*, 1913–1915

Anne Marie found all of this work deeply fulfilling, yet it also troubled her to an extent. While the material goods and spiritual lessons helped, they didn't necessarily provide long-term solutions. They were more like bandages than permanent remedies. Anne Marie knew she needed a deeper and more holistic solution, one that educated people so they could work and support themselves. This vital insight would soon become the basis for her entire life's work.

DETERMINING THE MISSION

After the French Revolution ended in 1799, Anne Marie's parents suggested she join the Sisters of Charity at Besançon. She agreed, but after trying it out she felt it wasn't a good fit. The order seemed too contemplative for the active and energetic saint, and she left the evening before her vows. Seeking a more practical outlet instead, she started a small school for girls. Yet again she faced problems. The local farmers saw little reason to educate their daughters and attendance fizzled out. The school closed, and like many young people today, Anne Marie was left wondering what to do with her life.

However, around this time she had a vision that seemed to provide an answer. One night while kneeling in prayer, she asked: "Lord, what would you have me do? Make your will known to me." She promised to do whatever God asked, no matter how difficult or terrifying. A voice answered her: "You will accomplish great things for me."[38]

A few nights later, disturbed from her sleep, she sat up and looked around, startled to see her room crowded with black, brown, and bronze children. The children reached toward her and cried out, "Dear Mother!" In the middle of the room stood a nun dressed in a strange habit. The nun said: "These are the children God has given you. He wishes you to form a new Congregation to care for them. I am Teresa. I will be your protectress."[39] Anne Marie later recognized the nun as St. Teresa of Ávila.

Now if you're like me, a room full of strange children, clawing and calling out, and a mysterious nun floating in their midst would cause nothing other than terror. But for Anne Marie, the vision crystallized her mission. She took it as a sign that God wanted her to educate the poor, especially children, helping them escape poverty by becoming productive citizens.

She and her three sisters immediately got to work. They started another small school, but this one grew quickly. Then they caught a lucky break when, in 1805, they discovered Pope Pius VII was passing through town. He was on his way back to Rome after Napoleon's coronation in Paris, and Anne Marie secured an audience. She recounted her dream, outlined her mission, and explained her desire to start a new community. Her vibrancy impressed the Pope, and when she asked for his blessing, he gave it, along with a word of encouragement: "Persevere in your vocation."[40]

As might be expected, the papal boost led to even more support. The local mayor gave Anne Marie a few former-seminary buildings for her work and also secured an annual grant from the town council. Within a short time the Javouhey children found themselves running several schools. Her brother operated the boys' school for 80 young men while she and her sisters educated over 120 girls. The success emboldened Anne Marie to finally carry out the mysterious nun's command. She appealed to the local bishop to start a new religious community, and with his approval on May 12, 1807, she and eight companions launched the Order of St. Joseph of Cluny. The young, active girl was now Mother Anne Marie Javouhey.

EXPANDING PARTICIPATION

"The nation's founders took daring steps to create structures of participation, mutual accountability, and widely distributed power to ensure the political rights and freedoms of all.... [S]imilar steps are needed today to expand economic participation, broaden the sharing of economic power, and make economic decisions more accountable to the common good."

— United States Catholic Bishops, *Economic Justice For All*, 297

WORLDWIDE EXPANSION

Over the following years, Anne Marie's organizational skills continued to shine. She opened new institutions throughout France: workshops, a hostel for the poor, another boys' school, a seminary, and community houses in other dioceses. But it was her educational endeavors that piqued the interest of the French government.

In 1814, she opened a school in Paris, using the English "Lancastrian" system to train its teachers. This involved training older student-leaders who then taught groups of ten. Many Parisians criticized the system for being foreign and, supposedly, leading to indifferentism. But Anne Marie just considered it a practical and efficient way to deal with teacher shortages. The French leaders agreed. They gave her control of a governmental school, encouraging her to apply the same methods, and then after her success they rewarded her with great acclaim. Almost overnight she became known throughout France as an expert educator.

Word spread far about the energetic and determined nun. Paris' ministry of the interior pitched her name to the governor of Réunion, a small French island off the southeast coast of Africa. The governor saw her educational system as a great way to help newly-emancipated slaves in French colonies, and so in 1817 he invited four of Anne Marie's sisters to start a school on the island. A few months later, he invited four more to launch a second one.

Officials from other countries took notice, too. The British governor of Gambia and Sierra Leone, two colonies in West Africa, invited Anne Marie to set up outposts in their areas. Anne Marie hesitated at first, because at the time, Gambia was a dumping ground for hundreds of foreign slaves. Worried about declining numbers, the government imported thirty prostitutes from London to increase the population. Dark moves like this crippled the community. Few citizens worked, theft was rampant, and slavery broke out among those who had once been slaves. Still, Anne Marie agreed to come. Working with the colony leaders, she created new systems of education, revamped the deplorable hospitals, and taught people the value of participating in society. The progress again impressed government leaders and led to more invitations.

PERSONAL FAITH, BUT NOT PRIVATE

Like Anne Marie Javouhey, Bl. Pier Giorgio Frassati was an energetic activist who brought his faith to the public square. He knew that while faith was personal it could never remain private. True faith always leads to public expression. Therefore, growing up in twentieth-century Italy, Pier Giorgio joined many political causes, speaking out most vigorously against Fascism. He was a prominent leader in the lay-run movement known as Catholic Action, which aimed to combat communistic and anti-clerical regimes.

One day, during a group protest in Rome, police forces converged and violently suppressed the activists. But Pier Giorgio rallied the young people by grabbing the group's banner, which police had knocked to the ground, and waving it high with pride and exuberance. We might see that moment as an icon for Pier Giorgio's faith: public, proud, effective, and deeply inspiring.

Pier Giorgio saw the value of public participation. He knew that society's progress depends on courageous men and women who stand up for what they believe in, who infuse society with the virtues of faith. While you and I might not raise physical banners in public squares, we can still follow Pier Giorgio's lead through other means like publishing blog posts and YouTube videos, rallying for good causes, and writing advocacy letters to our local newspaper. These small acts often lead to real and positive change.

FRENCH GUIANA

Finally, in 1828, Anne Marie began the adventure for which she's best known. Again at the invitation of the French government, she sailed to French Guiana, a colony on the upper coast of South America. The French had failed several times at colonizing the lush country. Considered by many too hot, too wet, too rugged, and too diseased for any productive development, the colony became overrun by convicts, thieves, and shady prospectors. A few years earlier, the French government tried to revive the colony by bringing in 160 tradesmen and farmers. By the time Anne Marie landed, that group had dwindled to just one family.

The savvy activist had no delusions about what she was getting into. On the voyage over, she stood in front of the 36 nuns and 86 laypeople accompanying her and warned, "I am taking you to Purgatory."[41]

But when she landed, the worries faded and the planning began. Anne Marie's goal was to create a new colony with local leaders, one more stable and self-supporting than prior attempts. New Angouleme, as she called it, would require all farmers and tradesmen to live a communal life. They would wake at 4:00 a.m. for Mass, work until 10:00 a.m. before the sun became too unbearable, and share meals together during the day. The nuns would educate all the local children — Europeans alongside Indian and African.

But then in 1831, as Anne Marie was still preparing the new colony, she received news that France passed a bill freeing all slaves. Word spread quickly, and within days, 600 slaves walked off their plantations in French Guiana toward the capital, Cayenne. When they arrived, they met an unprepared government. Knowing that immediate liberation would financially devastate the colonies, French leaders imposed a seven-year probation period during which the slaves could "prove" their suitability for freedom. In the meantime, as they had done so many times before, leaders turned to the one person they knew could help, a woman who successfully taught slaves for years, and established several flourishing communities.

Thus, in 1835, Anne Marie accepted her most remarkable and challenging assignment. Six hundred slaves needed to be prepared for emancipation and trained in the ways of civil society. She proposed they start a new colony at Mana, a nearby plateau, one with well-planned streets, a chapel, a clinic, a convent for nuns, and a dormitory for unmarried women. More importantly, she wanted to ensure a smooth transition for the slaves. As each family was liberated into the new colony, Anne Marie arranged to provide them some money, a small cottage with a garden, and a plot of land beyond the town to raise crops. She also convinced the government to dig irrigation channels and plant bananas and rice so that when the freed men and women arrived at their new farms, they would already be producing crops.

Finally, the day arrived. On May 21, 1838, wary leaders emancipated 185 slaves. The first thing many of them did was express their gratitude to Anne Marie. They handed her their charters of freedom since she was the one person they trusted. As one of them admitted: "We are free now, but we will never be free from the debt we owe you. We can only repay you with this promise: you will never be ashamed of us."[42]

To the surprise of local leaders, that promise held true. The initial 185 slaves smoothly transitioned into society, and over the next three years, Anne Marie helped three hundred more do the same. Crime was virtually absent in the Mana colony despite no policemen. All adults could read, most could write, and children filled the schools. The French leaders could not have been more pleased.

In 1843, after several successful years running the colony, she finally had to return to France. It was a sad farewell. As her ship sailed away, bobbing canoes surrounded the vessel, filled with free men and women saluting her and thanking her with song.

I like to think that as Anne Marie sailed away, she remembered her earlier vision. There around her, just as prophesied, sat black, brown, and bronze people, all crying out to her, "Dear Mother!"

From Senegal to Sierra Leone, Gambia to India, New Angouleme to Mana, Anne Marie traveled the world, serving and helping those in need. Of course, she didn't do it alone. She had sisters, coworkers, and constant support from the French government. But her activism and organizational skills helped Anne Marie become, in the words of Pope Pius XI, "the first woman missionary," a model saint for public participation.[43]

LESSONS FROM BL. ANNE MARIE JAVOUHEY

We can learn several lessons from Anne Marie's life. First, the value of solving problems instead of lamenting them. Anne Marie may not have heard the popular adage, "Don't complain about things you're unwilling to fix," but she certainly lived it. Whenever she saw a need, her first instinct was to dive in and help solve it whether related to education, medicine, or social service.

Our world has no fewer problems than Anne Marie's, and no shortage of analysts decrying them. But what we need is more people like her who choose to roll up their sleeves and get to work on finding the best ways to

A MORAL OBLIGATION

"In the Catholic Tradition, responsible citizenship is a virtue, and participation in political life is a moral obligation. This obligation is rooted in our baptismal commitment to follow Jesus Christ and to bear Christian witness in all we do. As the *Catechism of the Catholic Church* reminds us, 'It is necessary that all participate, each according to his position and role, in promoting the common good. This obligation is inherent in the dignity of the human person.... As far as possible citizens should take an active part in public life' (CCC 1913–1915)."

— *Forming Consciences for Faithful Citizenship*, #13

solve them. Next time we find ourselves griping about a particular issue, we can ask: "What steps am I taking, even if small, to help fix this?"

Second, Anne Marie provides a model for political participation. In her case, this meant directly working with the French government. The partnership led to several flourishing communities and educated thousands of poor citizens. For us, things might look different. Most of us won't have opportunities like hers — I'm not expecting the President to invite me to start a new colony — but we can affect our community through other ways, especially voting. In their document *Forming Consciences for Faithful Citizenship*, the American bishops teach that all Catholics have not only the right but the *duty* to participate in public life: "Responsible citizenship is a virtue, and participation in political life is a moral obligation."[44] By taking our voting duties seriously — both national and local — we can make a real impact.

Third, Anne Marie's work exhibits the power of enabling others to shape their own destinies. Anne Marie didn't want liberated slaves to fall prey to new forms of slavery, such as financial dependence. So she arranged a home and plot of land so they could personally affect their own flourishing.

One way to follow her lead today is by participating in micro-finance projects. Many charities like Catholic Relief Services (CRS) and Kiva.org allow donors to browse stories of third-world entrepreneurs looking for a little seed money to lift themselves out of poverty. For instance, we might find a baker from Tanzania who needs some pots and pans. Or we might encounter a Mexican seamstress who needs a small supply of cloth. When we give micro-donations through charities like these — usually somewhere between $5–$20 — we equip hardworking men and women to lift themselves out of poverty by their own chosen path. We provide not only money but the gift of participating in their own destiny.

Finally, we learn from Anne Marie the benefits and limitations of government service. Without the urging and support of the French government, Anne Marie could not have pulled off her many projects. It's doubtful, for example, that she could have started the new colonies for liberated slaves all by herself. At the same time, the government needed her just as much. As a large and bureaucratic institution it could not provide Anne Marie's spiritual nourishment and personal, dignifying love. Her example shows that we should avoid two extremes, one thinking the government is the answer to all our problems, the other thinking that it plays no role in solving any of them. Civil institutions play crucial roles in building a "civilization of love," but they can never replace private citizens, public organizations, religious groups, and most importantly, Jesus Christ.

RIGHTS AND RESPONSIBILITIES

The Catholic tradition teaches that human dignity can be protected and a healthy community can be achieved only if human rights are protected and responsibilities are met. **Therefore, every person has a fundamental right to life and a right to those things required for human decency.** Corresponding to these rights are duties and responsibilities — to one another, to our families, and to the larger society.

CHAPTER 5
ST. ROQUE
GONZÁLEZ

Born in 1576 in Asunción, the capital of Paraguay, Roque González was blessed with unique parents. His father was a conquistador, a bold adventurer who left Spain to conquer and colonize the New World. His mother, according to some accounts, was part Indian. She taught Roque the language of the Guarani, a local Indian tribe, a gift that would prove extremely helpful to his later missionary work.

During his early years, however, few people imagined Roque as a missionary. Everyone assumed the quiet and pious child would become a parish priest. He was an unusually good boy with a keen religious sense, praying constantly and preferring silence to games. When friends and family urged him toward the priesthood, Roque hesitated, feeling too unworthy and unsure. But eventually they convinced him, and in 1599, at age 23, he became Fr. Roque.

THE SECRET TO PEACE

"The secret to true peace resides in its respect for human rights."

— St. John Paul II,
Message for 32nd World Day of Peace

ENCOMIENDA SYSTEM

The political climate deeply shaped Roque's priesthood. At the time of his ordination, the Spanish and Portuguese conquest of South America was nearly complete. Conquistadors, armed with guns and horses, and driven by lust for gold, land, and power, established their reign throughout Paraguay.

UNIVERSAL, INVIOLABLE, AND INALIENABLE RIGHTS

"The ultimate source of human rights is not found in the mere will of human beings, in the reality of the State, in public powers, but in man himself and in God his Creator. These rights are "universal, inviolable, inalienable." *Universal* because they are present in all human beings, without exception of time, place, or subject. *Inviolable* insofar as they are inherent in the human person and in human dignity and because it would be vain to proclaim rights, if at the same time everything were not done to ensure the duty of respecting them by all people, everywhere, and for all people. *Inalienable* insofar as no one can legitimately deprive another person, whoever they may be, of these rights, since this would do violence to their nature."

— *Compendium of the Social Doctrine of the Catholic Church*, 153

The conquerors weren't wholly malicious. To their credit, and unlike other subjugators, Spanish leaders enacted laws meant to protect the dignity of those they overcame, namely the native Indians. They prohibited slavery, and they created new policies meant to encourage respectful Spanish settlements. Of these, the new *encomienda* system proved the most popular — but also the most controversial. Under this set-up, Spain offered colonists and conquistadors large plots of land, which would be held in trust for, and eventually turned over to, the Indians. For their part, the *encomenderos* agreed to protect the Indians, arrange for their education, and instruct them in Christianity. In return, the natives paid the *encomenderos* in the form of taxes and labor.

Though it may have been a well-intentioned system, it quickly grew corrupt. Many *encomenderos* forced their Indians into grueling labor without rest, and treated them essentially as slaves. Even worse, they turned a blind eye to Portuguese slave-hunters who raided the *encomiendas*, captured thousands of Indians, and then sold them into slavery. For an accurate depiction of the oppression, view the 1986 film *The Mission*. Though the events take place 150 years after Roque's time, they vividly capture the Indians' persecution.

Upon his ordination, Roque became gravely troubled by the *encomienda* system, and he wasn't the only one with reservations. A few decades before, Bartolomé de Las Casas, himself a successful *encomendero*, was so shocked by the abuses he witnessed that he renounced his land and freed his Indian slaves. He later became a Dominican priest and a passionate champion of justice for the Indians. During Bartolomé's time, many leaders argued that the Indians were less than human and needed Spanish colonists in order to become civilized. Bartolomé vehemently disagreed, maintaining that they were fully human and deserved the same rights as everyone else — especially the right of freedom. Bartolomé made numerous trips to the Spanish court to argue his case. In 1515, he met personally with King Charles V, the Holy Roman Emperor. The king surprisingly agreed with Bartolomé and decided to promulgate more humane laws. Pope Leo X later followed suit, officially condemning the enslavement of Indians. Yet, unfortunately, Madrid and Rome were thousands of miles from America, and most colonists ignored the interventions of the king and pope.

REDUCTIONS AND INCREASES

What particularly disturbed Roque, besides the civil rights abuses, was that the colonists' greed and violence hampered his ability to evangelize. The constant oppression convinced the Indians that Christ and slavery went hand-in-hand. Roque had to spend much of his early priesthood overcoming this misconception. One thing that helped was his unique heritage. Since Roque was a native-born Paraguayan, he didn't bear the stigma of European oppressors. And when he began speaking the Guarani language, they counted him as one of their own. Both traits caused many Indians to warmly welcome him as a friend.

In 1603, the local bishop assigned Roque to become rector of the cathedral at Asunción. This was normally a great honor, but in Roque's case, a sign that powerful colonists, frustrated by his opposition to the *encomienda* system, pressed for his transfer. For six years Roque served the cathedral with great devotion. However, when rumors began swirling that the bishop wanted to make him vicar-general, he decided to join the Jesuits because they typically eschewed high leadership positions. Even more, the Jesuits were leaders in caring for the Indians and Roque saw the order as an ideal way to carry out his mission.

The Jesuits also provided Roque an innovative strategy for serving the Indians. In opposition to the corrupt *encomienda* system the Jesuits implemented a series of *reducciones*, small, self-sufficient communities meant to fulfill, not suppress, the Indians' natural rights. (Unfortunately, the Spanish word *reduccion* transliterates into English as reduction, leading to confusion. But while the Spanish verb *reducir* normally means "reduce," here it means "gather into settled communities.")[45]

In these small villages, which excluded all European settlers, the Jesuits acted as trustees and guardians — not masters or bosses. They taught Indians how to govern themselves and arrange political institutions. The Indians learned to read, write, and sing, and artistic ability was encouraged.

The reductions were typically set up in a fertile plain on or near a river and followed a basic pattern. On one side of a central plaza would be the church, the priest's house, a house for widows and orphans, the cemetery, shops, and work spaces. On the other side were the Indians' homes. The Jesuits introduced to them a combination of collective and private ownership. The community farmed the main crops together but maintained their own animals and private gardens. Each self-governing reduction averaged 3,000 people, and, at their peak, between thirty and fifty existed throughout Paraguay.[46]

After joining the Jesuits, Roque poured himself into developing these reductions. In 1611, he established the reduction of San Ignacio Guazú, named for St. Ignatius of Loyola, in a fertile area between two rivers. He described the community in a letter to his Jesuit superior:

"The countryside near this little town is quite charming, and the climate is excellent, not nearly so apt to cause illness as are some other areas. The fields are fertile, widespread, and large enough to keep some four hundred farmers busy. There is no lack of water and firewood. Nearby forests offer opportunities for hunting, and all sorts of wild animals are plentiful. All this makes it easy for the Indians to forget about fishing, their main occupation in their homeland....

"Last year there was already something of a harvest. This year there is an abundance, which makes the people very happy. In this town there are some three hundred families, and in the vicinity some four hundred others, enough for another town....

"A church and parish house are being erected for our needs. Comfortable and enclosed with an adobe wall, the houses are built with cedar girders — cedar is very common wood here. We have worked hard to arrange all this. But with even greater zest and energy — in fact with all our strength — we have worked to build temples to Our Lord, not only those made by hands but spiritual temples as well, namely the souls of these Indians.

"On Sundays and feast days we preach during mass, explaining the catechism beforehand with equal concern for boys and girls. The adults are instructed in separate groups of about 150 men and the same number of women. Shortly after lunch, we teach them reading and writing for about two hours.

"There are still many non-Christians in this town. Because of the demands of planting and harvesting, all cannot be baptized at the same time. So every month we choose those best prepared for baptism. Among the 120 or so adults baptized this year there were several elderly shamans."[47]

Roque remained in charge of the San Ignacio reduction for three years, and then spent the rest of his life establishing other reductions. Fighting against hunger, cold, and exhaustion; swimming across rivers; wading through bogs; and fending off plaguing insects, Roque served the Indians heroically. He lived with them, ate their food, and shared in their work. He promoted their dignity, increased their self-esteem, and affirmed their inviolable rights. Roque's work was so remarkable that he impressed even non-Christians, like the French skeptic Voltaire:

"[T]he Paraguayan missions … had arrived at what is perhaps the highest degree of civilization to which it is possible to lead a young people…. In those missions, law was respected, morals were pure, a happy brotherliness bound men together, the useful arts and even some of the more graceful sciences flourished, and there was abundance everywhere."[48]

THE MOST BASIC RIGHT

In his encyclical *Christifideles Laici*, Pope St. John Paul II lists several fundamental rights including the right to a house and to work, to a family and responsible parenthood, to participate in public and political life, and to freedom of conscience and the practice of religion. But he also notes that the most important right, which grounds all others, is the right to life:

"The common outcry [on behalf of human rights] is false and illusory if the right to life, the most basic and fundamental right and the condition for all other personal rights, is not defended with maximum determination."[49]

Gianna Beretta Molla (1922–1962) had this in mind when her doctors offered her three choices, none of them good. It was during her second month of pregnancy and doctors announced they had found a tumor on her uterus. They could try to remove the tumor, which would produce dangerous complications. They could perform a hysterectomy, which would save Gianna's life but take the unborn child's and prevent further pregnancies. Or they could procure an abortion, which would allow future pregnancies but kill her unborn child.

Though Catholic moral teaching would have allowed the hysterectomy, Gianna exercised heroic virtue and chose to protect the life of her unborn child. Clear about her wishes, she told family and friends: "It will be a difficult delivery, and they may have to save one or the other — I want them to save my baby."[50]

Doctors removed the tumor and six months later Gianna gave birth to a healthy baby girl. Yet sadly, after just one week, Gianna fell ill and died from complications related to the tumor. She was just 39 years old.

On May 24, 2004, Pope John Paul II canonized Gianna Molla and celebrated her commitment to life. Both Gianna's husband, Pietro, and their daughter, Laura, were present at the canonization ceremony, the first time in Church history that a husband witnessed his wife's canonization.

OPPOSITION

Opposition runs through the lives of the saints as a common thread. And Roque's extraordinary influence and service did not exempt him. Spanish authorities tried to squeeze their way into the reductions by demanding each new community have a civil representative. When Roque denied their efforts, he created not a few enemies. Also, colonists and conquistadors became enraged as the reductions deprived them of valuable labor and supplies. The fact that Roque condemned their *encomienda* system as slavery probably didn't help either.

In 1614, as the opposition reached a tipping point, Roque courageously wrote a letter to his brother Francisco, the lieutenant governor of Paraguay's largest city, who sided with the *encomenderos*:

"I [understand] the strong feeling and complaints you have regarding the Indians and especially the feelings you have against us.

This is nothing new, nor anything that started yesterday. The *encomendero* gentlemen and soldiers have long complained and even gone further by stirring up strong opposition to the Society of Jesus. This, in fact, is a great honor to us.

I say this because the cause of the Indians is so just and because they have and have had a right to be free from the harsh slavery and forced labor called personal service. Indeed, they are exempt from this by natural law, both divine and human."[51]

We don't have Francisco's reply to Roque, but we know Roque's appeal greatly affected him. Just two months after Roque's letter, Francisco officially authorized his brother to establish several more reductions and forbade anyone from impeding their development.

From 1615 to 1627, Roque established reductions in Paraguay, southern Brazil, northeastern Argentina, and Uruguay. Desperately needing support, he received aid in 1628 when two Spanish Jesuits joined him, Juan de Castillo and Alonso Rodriguez (not to be confused with Alphonsus Rodriguez, the holy doorkeeper who mentored St. Peter Claver). The two men were twenty years younger than Roque but were experienced missionaries.

Together, the trio established two reductions near the southern tip of Brazil. But in doing so, they roused the ire of a local medicine man named Nezú. Nezú, an influential witch doctor, convinced his followers that all Jesuits in his territory had to be killed, and sent henchman to carry out the deed. On November 15, 1628, assassins entered one of the reductions. They found Roque hanging a bell in the new church, and, surprising him from behind, killed him with a single tomahawk-blow to the head. Alonso heard the commotion and rushed out the door. But the henchmen pounced and killed him, too. After the murders, the henchmen dragged their two bodies to the wooden chapel and set it on fire. Over the next month Nezú's men hunted down and killed four more Jesuit missionaries, including Juan de Castillo.

FATHER OF US ALL

During his extraordinary life, Roque González played a key role in one of the most effective social justice movements in Church history. He stood up for the rights of Indians when most everyone else wanted to exploit them. And he and his Jesuit brothers built over thirty reductions, each housing two to four thousand Indians. By the time the Jesuits were expelled from Paraguay in 1768, the reductions were home to about 80,000 people.[52]

Within six months of Roque's martyrdom, Church leaders opened his cause for canonization, by which he would officially be recognized as a saint. They collected testimony from his brother Jesuits, and from local Indians, including these words from Chief Guarecupi: "All the Christians among my countrymen loved the Father [Roque] and grieved for his death, because he was the father of us all, and so he was called by the Indians of the Parana."[53]

Unfortunately, most of the canonization documents were lost while being delivered to Rome, and the cause slowed to a halt. But in 1934, copies of the originals unexpectedly turned up, and upon review Pope Piux XI beatified Roque González with his two Jesuit counterparts — Alonso Rodriguez and Juan de Castillo. Pope John Paul II then canonized the trio in 1988.

LESSONS FROM ST. ROQUE GONZÁLEZ

From this premiere social justice hero we can learn several lessons. First, Roque shows that when discerning our calling, we should consider our unique skills and opportunities. For example, perhaps we can speak a language other friends can't. I live in Florida, where many Hispanic immigrants desperately need help. I don't speak Spanish, making it tough for me to serve them. However, many of my friends do, and by recognizing their unique linguistic abilities, they've chosen to minister to the Hispanic population.

In Roque's case, his father passed down an adventurous, missionary spirit while his mother bequeathed a serene sensitivity, and taught Roque the language of a local Indian tribe. Being born in Paraguay also placed Roque in the right location for his work. When Roque surveyed these unique gifts — his zeal, his linguistic abilities, his geography — he quickly sensed where and whom to serve. Like him, we can uncover our unique paths by considering our own gifts, culture, and family heritage.

Second, Roque shows us that we can best protect the rights of marginalized people by first identifying with them. Roque was able to help the Guarani Indians, in particular, because he spoke their language and learned their culture. He grew close to them, eating their food, living in their houses, and sharing their pains. This gave him firsthand experience of the tragic injustices they suffered and energized him to find a solution. In the same way, we might seek to identify with people we're helping.

Third, Roque teaches us to love our oppressors — even firmly, when necessary. Anytime we stand up for human rights, we'll run into opposition. We'll encounter people who benefit from suppressing others' rights and who therefore resist any change. Yet look how Roque handled those who disagreed with his service. In the letter to his brother Francisco, he expressed understanding for the *encomenderos* while not giving up on their conversion. This doesn't mean he was soft about their repentance. Roque's love was strong but firm. He denied *encomenderos* the sacrament of confession until they stopped oppressing the Indians, and he publicly condemned their behavior.

But as much as he wanted to liberate the Indians, Roque wanted to win his enemies to the right side of justice. The civil rights giant Martin Luther King, Jr., expressed this same desire beautifully in his 1957 sermon, "Love Your Enemies":

"Love has within it a redemptive power. And there is a power there that eventually transforms individuals.... They react with guilt feelings, and sometimes they'll hate you a little more at that transition period, but just keep loving them. And by the power of your love they will break down under the load. That's love, you see. It is redemptive, and this is why Jesus says love. There's something about love that builds up and is creative. There is something about hate that tears down and is destructive. So love your enemies."[54]

We can follow Roque's path by fighting vigorously against injustice while also loving our enemies and oppressors toward the truth.

CHAPTER 6

ST. THOMAS MORE

Over the last few decades, we've seen an increasing number of attacks on religious liberty. In the United States, many Catholic organizations are no longer free to live by their most deeply held beliefs. Throughout the rest of the world, believers are targeted and slaughtered because of their faith. In these times when we can no longer take religious freedom for granted, many Catholics have turned to the example of St. Thomas More.

We venerate Thomas for following his beliefs, even in the face of persecution. The 1966 film *A Man for All Seasons* — which won Oscars for Best Picture and Best Actor — introduced millions of people to his courage. He knew that among his many responsibilities, including caring for his family and the poor of England, his chief duty was to serve the truth.

Thomas was just twelve years old when he left home for Lambeth Palace in 1490. John Morton, the kind archbishop of Canterbury and Lord Chancellor of England, had known Thomas' dad for years. Over time, he took an interest in the gifted boy and invited him to study at the palace.

When Thomas arrived on the first day, a host led him back to the servant's quarters, where he would live during his studies. An early dinner sat waiting. Thomas sat down alongside other youths, pages like himself, and they immediately began peppering him with questions: "Who are you? How old are you? Where are you from? What does your father do? Tell us about yourself!"

Although taken aback, Thomas answered each query with great excitement. He had always been cheerful and delighted to make new friends. He didn't realize, though, that as he spoke, the boys took turns swiping his food. By the time he finished speaking he looked down at an empty plate. The boy next to him smiled with bulging cheeks. "That'll teach you to talk so much!" he chuckled. Thomas could only grin, for he appreciated a good joke as much as anyone.[55]

Before he had time to find any more food, the head steward rushed in to announce the archbishop and his guests were ready for dinner. The pages leapt up and headed for the kitchen, where they emerged carrying large plates of food. Thomas felt very hungry at the sight of rich soups, river fish, kidneys cooked in wine, and several types of meat. He stood longingly near the table, admiring the rich food, and let out a long sigh.

Suddenly, the man in front of him perked up: "Well, now, and who is this blowing down my neck?" The words snapped Thomas out of his trance. In panic he recognized the man in front of him was the archbishop.

"I didn't mean any harm," said the startled Thomas, "I — I was just interested."

"And there's certainly no harm in that," agreed the archbishop. "Only, the next time you blow, warn me beforehand, and I'll pull up my fur collar!" He smiled at Thomas and continued, "You must be the son of my good friend, Sir John More?"

"Yes, sir — I mean, My Lord," Thomas said, "I've come here to learn."

One of the other guests replied, "And I expect a bright lad like you has learned a thing or two already! What have you learned today, boy?"

Thomas smiled. "Please, sir, I've learned that I must eat my dinner very fast indeed, or someone will finish it for me."[56]

All the guests burst with laughter. Over the following months, Thomas became known for his cleverness and humor. He also developed a reputation for charity. One day, Thomas' childhood nurse visited the palace and brought along a basket of sumptuous cakes. They chatted happily for many hours, but as Thomas saw her out of the palace, he returned through the kitchen, running into a large crowd of poor servants. Men, women, and children huddled around bare scraps of food.

Thomas knew how it felt to be hungry. So he quickly untied the cloth bundle in his hands and passed out the cakes. It marked a key moment in his life. From then on, he considered it his responsibility to care for the poor.[57]

Over the next two years, Thomas became the best student in the palace. He mastered Latin and impressed Archbishop Morton so much that he decided to send Thomas off to study at Oxford University. The opportunity thrilled Sir John More. He wanted his son to become a lawyer like himself, and Oxford was a great training ground. But Thomas had other plans in mind. While at school, he gravitated toward theology and Greek studies. Also, since many of his fellow students were on track to become priests or monks, Thomas wondered whether he too had a religious vocation. When his father discovered these interests he immediately summoned Thomas home to London.

Sir John enrolled Thomas at New Inn, one of the more famous English courts. There Thomas obeyed his father's will and pursued law. He excelled at school, as usual, passing his exams with high honors. He became a lawyer, as his father desired, and began taking on heavy case loads, especially on behalf of the poor. For several years he worked tirelessly standing up for people who society treated unjustly.

DUTIES AND RESPONSIBILITIES

"We also have a duty to secure and respect these rights not only for ourselves, but for others, and to fulfill our responsibilities to our families, to each other and to the larger society."

— USCCB, *Faithful Citizenship*, 14

THE HIGH COST OF RESPONSIBILITY

Then, in 1504, Thomas received exciting news. Townspeople elected the twenty-six-year-old lawyer a member of the House of Commons. This allowed him to exercise even more influence for the cause of justice.

However, his excitement quickly tempered. The king at the time, Henry VII, was a wise but greedy ruler. And the older Henry grew, the more riches he demanded. Every few years, he ordered Parliament to pass new taxes to pay for his lavish parties. The year Thomas entered parliament, King Henry asked for a 113,000-pound grant (about $86 million today!).

The members of Parliament balked at the exorbitant sum. But nobody dared stand up against the king — nobody, that is, except young Thomas. When the debate landed on the floor of Parliament, it went mostly in the king's favor. But then Thomas defiantly rose and argued so persuasively against the proposal that he won over the entire House of Commons. In the end, they still awarded King Henry 30,000 pounds, but it was far less than the king's original request.

When the news reached King Henry, he became enraged. He immediately ordered that Thomas be executed, though his councilors calmed him down. Instead, Henry figured the safest way to take vengeance, while avoiding public outcry, was through his father. King Henry had Sir John arrested and imprisoned at the Tower of London, where he would stay indefinitely.

Thomas learned a valuable lesson from the experience. He figured his defiance would bring consequences, sure, but he never thought they would lead to his guiltless father's imprisonment. The episode revealed that standing up for what is right, and being responsible to the truth, often brings great difficulty, both to you and those you love. Difficult choices force us to choose between our comfort and reputation, and what we know is right. Thomas carried this lesson with him through the next major phase of his life, which included another struggle with another King Henry.

THE KING'S GREAT MATTER

King Henry VII died on April 22, 1509, and his son, Henry VIII, succeeded him. The new king noticed Thomas' influence, which continued to grow. In 1510, Thomas served as one of two undersheriffs in London, where he developed a reputation for honesty and responsibility. In 1514, the king appointed him Privy Councilor, making Thomas one of his closest advisers. In

A SHEPHERD RESPONSIBLE FOR HIS FLOCK

St. Thomas More was not afraid to stand up for what is right, and neither was Bl. Vilmos Apor (1892–1945). As the bishop of Gyor, Hungary, during World War II, he found himself in the middle of one of the deadliest assaults in history. Yet even in such danger, he constantly put others' rights ahead of his own. During air raids, he was known for opening his house to those whose homes had been destroyed. On Holy Saturday, 1945, Russian troops barged into his episcopal residence and demanded that 100 women be taken from there to their own barracks. He flatly refused. A Russian officer shot and wounded him, and he died three days later.

Bl. Vilmos took seriously his responsibility as a shepherd. During his beatification, Pope John Paul II summed up his character: "He was not fearful about raising his voice, in accord with evangelical principles, to denounce injustice and abuse against minorities, especially against the Jewish community."[58]

1523, the House of Commons elected Thomas its Speaker. Then in 1529, the king promoted Thomas to Lord Chancellor of England, the first layman ever to hold the position. The new role effectively made Thomas the second most powerful man in all of England.

Thomas didn't really want the position. He knew it would consume more time and create new enemies. But he also felt responsible to serve his country in whatever way necessary. It helped that Thomas and Henry enjoyed a strong friendship, as the two had known each other since boyhood. Thomas had always appreciated the King's joviality and kindness. Henry admired Thomas' commitment to justice and his concern for the rights of others. But after Thomas became Lord Chancellor, their friendship would become rocky.

Their main conflict surrounded Henry's marriage to Queen Catherine of Aragon. Thomas greatly respected Catherine, who was a kind and devout woman. But King Henry soured on her when she proved unable to produce a male heir. At the same time, Henry fell in love with Anne Boleyn, one of Catherine's servant girls. By early 1526, the king's one desire was to annul his marriage to Catherine and marry Anne. He even convinced himself that God had cursed his marriage with Catherine, preventing them from having male children, and therefore believing his annulment was divinely prescribed.

The local bishops, afraid to contradict the king, quickly agreed. Henry then appealed directly to Pope Clement VII. The Pope, however, offered no support.

King Henry became angry and lashed out. He ordered Thomas to announce, in front of Parliament, new reforms to the Church of England. The command made Thomas extremely uneasy. He knew Henry's idea of reform would be far different than his own.

And he was right. After the Pope refused to support the king's marriage, Henry decided to attack the English bishops and all the Pope's supporters.

He first demanded a huge fine from the English clergy and ordered them to accept King Henry as "Sole Protector and Supreme Head of the Church and Clergy in England." This, in effect, would make him Pope of England. Almost all of the bishops complied, though they were able to qualify the title by adding "so far as the law of God allows."

But Thomas didn't agree, and he was horrified that so many bishops caved in. He couldn't believe the king would place himself in authority over the Church. In protest, he tried to resign from being Lord Chancellor, but King Henry refused to accept.

On May 15, 1532, the English bishops officially handed the king all the authority of the Church in England. The next morning, Thomas More arrived at the king's office and offered, once again, his resignation, this time citing health problems. Though the king was skeptical and knew the real reason Thomas wanted to leave, he accepted. The two men parted on friendly terms, though King Henry boiled with resentment. It was only a matter of time until his wrath fell on Thomas.

RESIGNATION AND REFUSAL TO TAKE OATH

Thomas' resignation reduced him and his household to near-poverty. He still had a pension, and a few small plots of land, but the Mores had to cut back on most expenses. They sold their extra property, dismissed their servants, and began eating dry bread and water — a far cry from the exquisite meals they had grown accustomed to.

At one point, the English bishops offered Thomas a large sum of money as a "reward" for his longtime service. But Thomas respectfully declined. He didn't want his adversaries to think he could be bribed. Friends and family couldn't understand why he turned it down, even when he explained that his conscience wouldn't allow it, and that if he was responsible to nothing else, he had to obey it. As he later wrote:

> "You must understand that, in things touching conscience, every true and good subject is more bound to have respect to his said conscience and to his soul than to any other thing in all the world."[59]

Thomas also turned down his invitation to the coronation of Queen Anne Boleyn. He knew the king would see his absence as a personal affront, and he did. But the new queen became outraged, believing Thomas intentionally insulted her. So in January 1534, at his new wife's request, King Henry issued a bill accusing Thomas of treason. But Thomas' popularity and lawyer skills came in handy and he persuaded Parliament to drop the charges.

BASIC RIGHTS AND BASIC DUTIES

"In human society one man's natural right gives rise to a corresponding duty in other men; the duty, that is, of recognizing and respecting that right. Every basic human right draws its authoritative force from the natural law, which confers it and attaches to it its respective duty."

— St. John XXIII, *Pacem en Terris* ("Peace on Earth"), 30

BUILDING WITH ONE HAND, DESTROYING WITH THE OTHER

"The mutual complementarities between rights and duties — they are indissolubly linked — are recalled several times.... Those, therefore, who claim their own rights, yet altogether forget or neglect to carry out their respective duties, are people who build with one hand and destroy with the other."

— *Compendium of the Social Doctrine of the Catholic Church*, 156

It was only a temporary reprieve, as one of his friends reminded him: "The anger of kings means death!"[60] But Thomas had cleverly avoided the king's wrath again.

About two weeks later, King Henry ratcheted up the pressure. He forced Parliament to pass an "Act of Succession," stating that Anne Boleyn's children would be heirs to the English throne. It also declared that Henry's first marriage had not been valid and that the Pope was not the head of the English Church. Though many people were shocked at such boldness, King Henry forced every Englishman over the age of twenty-one to sign an oath, swearing they agreed with the Act.

Naturally, Thomas refused to sign. When asked why not, he chose to remain silent, knowing that silence could not be construed as treason. Thomas was a lawyer and understood how far he could go in opposing the king. He relied on the the legal precedent *qui tacet consentire videtur*, meaning "who [is] silent is seen to consent." He knew King Henry could not convict him as long as he did not explicitly deny the king's authority over the Church.

But eventually the king got his way. He had Thomas arrested on Sunday, April 12, 1534, right after Mass. Guards led Thomas to Lambeth palace, where he had joyfully studied as a young boy. There waited Archbishop Thomas Cranmer, one of the king's key supporters, who asked Thomas to sign the oath.

Thomas could no longer remain silent: "I cannot sign this."

"And why not, Mr. More?" demanded the archbishop.

"Because I don't agree to it. I'll certainly agree that the children of King Henry and Queen Anne are to inherit the English throne. But this oath makes me agree to other things as well. I can't sign it."

"You must obey the orders of your king!" shouted Archbishop Cranmer.

"Before anything," Thomas corrected, "I must obey my conscience."[61]

When word reached the king, he became furious. His patience with Thomas had reached its end. He ordered Thomas to the Tower of London, where Thomas knew that few prisoners came out alive. Yet he remained firm, unafraid, and committed to following his conscience, even if it led to death.

THE KING'S GOOD SERVANT — BUT GOD'S FIRST

Thomas sat in prison for more than a year. Then finally, on July 1, 1535, guards summoned him to Westminster Hall for his long-awaited trial. The king had appointed a one-sided tribunal to convict Thomas of treason. It included Anne Boleyn's father, brother, and uncle, and they were determined to convict Thomas even without sufficient evidence. By the end, most jurors knew Thomas was innocent. But they also knew what verdict Henry VIII expected. They deliberated for only fifteen minutes before reaching their decision: "Guilty."

Thomas embraced his death sentence with great calm and composure. He rose to address the crowd around him, and began by complimenting the king, with whom he disagreed but still liked:

"I owe His Grace much for all the favors he has done for me. I'm particularly grateful to King Henry for having had me shut up here all these months. It's given me a chance to prepare myself for death."[62]

On July 6, guards told Thomas he was to die that day. He put on his best clothes and was led out of the dark Tower for the last time. The sun blazed over the execution hill as he climbed the scaffold. Looking down at the large crowd, he asked for their prayers, and then declared:

"I am dying for our Catholic faith, good people. And I call you to witness that I die the king's loyal servant — but God's first."[63]

The ever-cheerful Thomas even calmed the nervous executioner with some wisecracks: "Cheer up, man, and don't mind doing your job. My neck is very short, so see you aim straight. You don't want to spoil your reputation!" The executioner lifted up his axe, ready for the final blow. Then Thomas cried: "Stop! I must put my beard aside. It would be a shame to chop it off. After all, my poor beard is not accused of treason."[64]

It was the last cheerful quip of many throughout his life. A second later, the axe fell and the crowd let up a loud sigh. Thomas More was dead.

LESSONS FROM ST. THOMAS MORE

The tremendous example of St. Thomas More offers several lessons about rights and responsibilities. First, he reminds us that we're all responsible for upholding the rights of others. When it comes to rights and duties, today's world usually gets one side of the equation right. We strongly emphasize our own rights, demanding the right to do what we want, say what we want, and live where we want. And none of this is inherently bad, for to an extent, Catholic social teaching would agree. The Church maintains a long list of basic rights that all people deserve to claim.

Yet along with those rights we have corresponding responsibilities. These duties root themselves in our common brotherhood, the fact that we're all created by the same God and are members of the same eternal family. This means we're responsible for helping each other flourish.

Thomas knew this well, and it explains why he consistently submitted his own wants to the needs of others: to the material needs of the poor, to the legal needs of the oppressed, and to the demands of truth and conscience. For every right we have, we have the duty to protect that right in others.

Second, Thomas shows us that accepting these duties can often lead to discomfort. Thomas was no fool. He knew that refusing to sign the oath honoring the king's Act of Succession would likely end in death. He sensed that family and friends would not understand, and that standing for the truth would cost his job, his home, and probably his life. But he also knew it was the right thing to do. He prayed near the end of his life:

"Give me, good Lord, a longing to be with you: not for the avoiding of the calamities of this wicked world, nor of the pains of hell."[65]

Thomas prepared himself for his final trial through a lifetime of small sacrifices. He regularly ate leftover scraps, giving his best food away to the poor. On many nights he slept on the floor, with a log for his pillow. These small acts of intentional discomfort trained him for the greater discomfort he suffered later on — imprisonment, isolation, and execution. We too can train ourselves so that when duty requires uncomfortable choices, we're ready to embrace them with heroic virtue.

Third, Thomas demonstrates that standing up for what is right doesn't have to be gloomy. Throughout his life, he responded to his many difficulties with smiles and good cheer. From his boyhood quips at Lambeth palace, to his lighthearted humor at his execution, Thomas answered St. Teresa of

Ávila's plea: "God protect me from gloomy faced saints." Our attitude often drives our ability to respond well to difficulties. If we're constantly cynical, or complain about every small hardship we suffer, we'll never develop the moral fiber needed to stand against truly formidable opposition. Thomas knew that laughing and joking diffused the darkness his trials threatened to bring, and it brightened the lives of people around him.

OPTION FOR THE POOR AND VULNERABLE

A basic moral test is how our most vulnerable members are faring. In a society marred by deepening divisions between rich and poor, our tradition recalls the story of the Last Judgment (Mt 25:31–46) and instructs us to put the needs of the poor and vulnerable first.[66]

CHAPTER 7
BL. PIER
GIORGIO
FRASSATI

As a fairly new Catholic in 2010, I wanted to learn more about the saints, so I devised a plan. On my twenty-fourth birthday, I would begin a year-long study focusing on one particular saint. One friend suggested I choose St. Lawrence of Rome, my confirmation saint. But there wasn't enough material to fill a whole year. Another friend recommended St. Thérèse of Lisieux, the magnanimous Little Flower who died when she was just 24, the same age I would be. I liked that connection, and settled on her.

But then a third friend introduced me to Bl. Pier Giorgio Frassati. Like Thérèse, Pier Giorgio died early at age 24. Also like the Little Flower, he displayed an impressive spiritual maturity. Yet I quickly discovered that beyond those two connections, the two saints could hardly be more different. Thérèse lived a contemplative life and pursued God within an obscure cloister. Pier Giorgio lived a dynamic and active life, climbing large mountains, protesting in the streets, and partying with friends.

I figured each saint would offer unique lessons so I adopted both that year. As expected, I learned plenty from Thérèse. She taught me the value of hidden sacrifices and her famed "little way" of holiness. But throughout the year, I grew especially fond of Pier Giorgio. He's now my favorite saint and, in fact, he's the inspiration for this book. If it only had one chapter, it would be about

THE BREAD OF THE HUNGRY

"The bread which you do not use is the bread of the hungry; the garment hanging in your wardrobe is the garment of him who is naked; the shoes that you do not wear are the shoes of the one who is barefoot; the money that you keep locked away is the money of the poor; the acts of charity that you do not perform are so many injustices that you commit."

— St. Basil the Great[67]

him. As you'll see, Pier Giorgio uniquely embodied the Church's social doctrine. He fused faith with charity, contemplation with activism, personal care with institutional reform, and boundless joy with the grit of service.

"THIS IS FOR YOU, JESUS!"

Pier Giorgio was born on April 6, 1901, to wealthy parents in Turin, Italy. His mother, Adelaide, was a painter who appreciated fine art and high culture. His father, Alfredo, owned and edited *La Stampa*, an influential Italian newspaper. He also became the youngest senator in Italy in 1913 and later served as the Italian ambassador to Germany.

The Frassatis were not deeply religious. Adelaide attended Mass regularly, but neither Pier Giorgio nor his younger sister, Luciana, ever saw her receive communion or kneel to pray.[68] Pier Giorgio's father was admittedly agnostic.

Yet his parents did exhibit high values. For instance, Alfredo strongly committed himself to justice, routinely taking courageous moral stands. He used his newspaper to advocate against Italy's entry into World War I and to regularly challenge Fascism, both stands coming at great personal cost.

The high moral environment in which Pier Giorgio was raised helped fuel his spiritual development. When he was about four years old, his tutor took him on an errand. Along the way, they encountered a priest processing through the streets with the Eucharist. The priest walked behind a handful of altar boys who led the way, carrying large candles and ringing bells. As was common in Italy at the time, people knelt on the street to honor Jesus. The tutor whispered to Pier Giorgio, "Our Lord is coming. Let us kneel down because he is a king." The precocious boy knelt and responded, "Yes, he is the King of kings!"

A few months later, at the annual Corpus Christi procession, Pier Giorgio stood on his balcony, looking down as the Eucharist moved slowly in procession. Other people leaned over their balconies and threw flowers. But Pier Giorgio realized he didn't have any, so he reached into the pocket of a relative and pulled out a nice gold pen. He threw it down to the road, shouting, "This is for you, Jesus!"

As he grew older, Pier Giorgio's faith continued to develop, and along with it a keen desire to serve others.

A LIVING OPTION FOR THE POOR

When Catholic social teaching encourages an "option for the poor and vulnerable," the word "option" does not mean "choice," as though Catholics can choose whether to serve the poor. Instead, it suggests "preference." Followers of Jesus Christ should always *prefer* the needs, concerns, and desires of poor and vulnerable people above their own. This means the first question we must ask of any action, purchase, or political decision is how it impacts those on the margins of society.

Pier Giorgio knew this well. He regularly made sacrifices to serve others. One morning when he was a young boy, a frail woman knocked on his door with a barefoot child in her arms. Pier Giorgio quickly removed his shoes and socks, gave them to her, and shut the door before anyone could object.[69]

THE FUNDAMENTAL MORAL CRITERION

"As followers of Christ, we are challenged to make a fundamental option for the poor — to speak for the voiceless, to defend the defenseless, to assess life styles, policies, and social institutions in terms of their impact on the poor....

"Decisions must be judged in light of what they do for the poor, what they do to the poor, and what they enable the poor to do for themselves. The fundamental moral criterion for all economic decisions, policies, and institutions is this: They must be at the service of all people, especially the poor."

— USCCB, *Economic Justice for All*, 16, 24

In 1918 at age 17, Pier Giorgio joined the St. Vincent de Paul Society. The Society centered itself on personal compassion more than faceless donations. When someone joined, he was assigned specific poor families to visit and care for. Pier Giorgio reveled in these visits. They were his chance to not only offer material support but also spiritual encouragement. His visits to jobless war veterans, destitute laborers, and homeless children lifted many spirits and became his daily passion. "I see a special light surrounding the poor and unfortunate," he observed to a friend, "a light that we do not have."[70]

As time went on, this service to the poor confounded his parents and friends. They couldn't fathom why a well-off boy would sacrifice comfort for others. A friend once asked Pier Giorgio why he traveled on trains in third-class when he could easily afford better. He replied: "I travel third because there isn't a fourth."[71]

When Pier Giorgio showed up late for dinner — a regular occurrence — his parents would become irate. But they didn't know he would run all the way home after giving away his train money. One night, when the temperature was twelve degrees below zero, Pier Giorgio arrived at home wearing a smile but no overcoat. His angry father demanded to know where his coat was. "I gave it away," Pier Giorgio explained. "You see, Dad, it was cold."[72]

When his sister, Luciana, got married, she shared with him 1,000 liras from her wedding gifts. Pier Giorgio gave 500 liras to the St. Vincent de Paul Society and the other 500 to his club, Cesare Balbo, which was part of the FUCI, the Italian Catholic Student Federation.[73] Later, his father gave him 5,000 liras instead of a car, and Pier Giorgio donated all of it to the new St. Vincent de Paul group in his parish.

By the time he was 21, he was personally helping several families. He made sure local children received the sacraments and sponsored many of them. Pier Giorgio helped one lady stay extra time in the maternity ward of a hospital. Later, he acted as godfather to her daughter, bought a dress for her baptism, and waited outside prison when the lady's husband was released, helping him find work in a factory that accepted people with prison records. We'll probably never know the full scope of Pier Giorgio's charity, most of which he accomplished without fanfare.

Pier Giorgio didn't focus only on individual charity. In line with Catholic social teaching, he also advocated for institutional justice. He liked to say, "Charity is not enough: we need social reform."[74] The young, zealous activist joined several movements and organizations, including Catholic Action and the Catholic Student Federation. He was an active member in the Italian Popular Party, protested against Mussolini's Fascist regime, and also helped found a Catholic daily newspaper called *Il Momento*, which was devoted to spreading the social principles of Pope Leo XIII's encyclical, *Rerum Novarum*. His social involvement went well beyond Italy's borders as he participated in the first international meeting of Pax Romana and consulted with Catholic activists in Germany and Austria.

TRUE TREASURES OF THE CHURCH

Persecution was a daily reality for third-century Christians in Rome. And in 258, the Emperor Valerian began another massive round. He issued an edict commanding that all bishops, priests, and deacons should be put to death, and he gave the Imperial treasury power to confiscate all money and possessions from Christians.

In light of the news, Pope Sixtus II quickly ordained a young Spanish theologian, Lawrence, to become archdeacon of Rome. The important position put Lawrence in charge of the Church's riches, and it gave him responsibility for the Church's outreach to the poor. The pope sensed his own days were numbered and therefore commissioned Lawrence to protect the Church's treasure.

On August 6, 258, Valerian captured Pope Sixtus while he celebrated the liturgy, and had him beheaded. Afterwards, he set his sights on the pope's young protégé, Lawrence. But before killing him, the Emperor demanded the archdeacon turn over all the riches of the Church. And he gave Lawrence three days to round it up.

Lawrence worked swiftly. He sold the Church's vessels and gave the money to widows and the sick. He distributed all the Church's property to the poor. On the third day, the Emperor summoned Lawrence to his palace and asked for the treasure. With great aplomb, Lawrence entered the palace, stopped, and then gestured back to the door where, streaming in behind him, poured crowds of poor, crippled, blind, and suffering people. "These are the true treasures of the Church," he boldly proclaimed. One early account even has him adding, "The Church is truly rich, far richer than the Emperor."

Unsurprisingly, Lawrence's act of defiance angered the Emperor. Valerian ordered his death that same day. Hundreds of year later, Lawrence is still remembered for his final jest: while being barbecued alive, he quipped to his executioners, "I'm well done. Turn me over!" But we should also hail Lawrence for his keen insight regarding the Church's real treasure.

CHARITY FUELED BY FAITH

A friend once asked Pier Giorgio how he could stand visiting the homes of poor people: "They're disgusting, filthy, and smelly. How can you tolerate that?"

Pier Giorgio responded: "Jesus comes to me every morning in Communion, and I return the visit by going to serve the poor."[75]

With that answer Pier Giorgio revealed the key to his remarkable option for the poor. His service flowed from an inner closeness to Christ. And that intimacy developed over the years through two spiritual poles: the Eucharist and prayer.

Pier Giorgio began attending daily Mass as a young boy, a practice he continued throughout the rest of his life. While visiting Pollone, at the family's country estate, he often headed out early in the morning and returned before anyone else awoke. And when he was planning to hike to the nearby

Sanctuary of Oropa, a shrine dedicated to Mary, he asked the gardener to wake him by pulling on a long rope tied to a table in his room. The rope was then draped out his window, and when the gardener tugged the rope, the table rattled, and Pier Giorgio hopped out of bed. One morning, however, the gardener pulled and pulled, and Pier Giorgio didn't wake, so he yanked extremely hard and toppled over the table. Pier Giorgio's mother rushed in and when he assured her that "it's nothing," she advised him to turn on the light next time so he wouldn't trip over things.[76]

Pier Giorgio was a skilled outdoorsman who loved to hike, but no matter how inconvenient, he made sure that his mountain excursions enabled him to attend Mass. If he wouldn't be able to attend Mass, he wouldn't go.

The other pole of Pier Giorgio's spirituality was prayer. A priest once asked him, "Is it true, Pier Giorgio, that when you are in your room you pray for a long time?" He didn't respond, so the priest continued, "Your mother told me so. You are upsetting her, and she gets up in the night...."

"But I have so many prayers to say," Pier Giorgio interrupted, to which the priest replied, "And who has ordered you to?" He answered: "No one. I just have to."[77]

Pier Giorgio always carried his rosary with him and he prayed it regularly. On his bedroom door he tacked St. Bernard's prayer to the Virgin from Dante's *Paradiso*: "Lady, you are so great and accessible, that anyone who wants grace and fails to ask your intercession, his desire tries to fly without wings."[78]

Pier Giorgio often spent hours meditating in prayer. Friends remember that he sometimes became so transfixed when praying in front of the Blessed Sacrament that he became oblivious to his surroundings. In one instance, some nearby candles melted causing hot wax to drip on his head, though Pier Giorgio didn't seem to notice at all. A friend had to shake him out of his prayerful bliss to prevent injury.[79]

"THIS IS YOUR HOME"

Since the start of his pontificate, Pope Francis has personified the "option for the poor and vulnerable." Many examples stand out, from embracing a disabled boy in St. Peter's Square to washing the feet of poor mothers or praying with poor families in the slums of Rio de Janeiro.

One of my favorite gestures took place on July 1, 2013. Pope Francis welcomed a group of 200 homeless men and women for dinner at the Vatican. A fellow cardinal greeted the guests saying, "This is your home, and [we are] pleased that you are here."

The guests then enjoyed food served by chefs from Naples and music from the Vatican Gendarmes Band. The Vatican spared no expense. Each person left with a gift bag packed with pastries, fresh fruit, and a rosary.

What Pope Francis carried out on a grand scale, we can easily do in our world. Whether we take a homeless person out for a hamburger, or invite a poor family from our parish over for dinner, sharing a meal is about more than just sharing food. It's about giving someone else preference over our time, money, and comfort. It's about affirming their incalculable dignity and taking a true "option" for the poor.

TO THE HEIGHTS!

Throughout his life, Pier Giorgio maintained a deep appreciation for skiing and mountain climbing. "Every day that passes I fall more and more in love with the mountains," he wrote to a friend. "If it weren't for my studies, I would spend entire days up in the pure mountain air, contemplating the greatness of the Creator."[80] For Pier Giorgio, the mountains offered an occasion to contemplate God and strengthen his spiritual life.

On June 7, 1925, he climbed a mountain for the last time. He had a friend take a picture near the top. On the back of the photo, Pier Giorgio wrote "*Verso l'alto!*" which means "Toward the top!" or "To the heights!" Little did he know how prophetic that message would become. Two weeks after the photo, Pier Giorgio contracted polio, likely through one of his poor or sick friends.

The disease acted quickly. In those days polio had no cure or vaccine, which led Pier Giorgio to experience severe, crippling pain and become essentially paralyzed within a few days. Yet even as he suffered, he kept the poor in mind. From his bed he asked his sister to deliver medicine to a sick friend and to renew a pawn receipt for a poor woman who had pawned her wedding ring.

Pier Giorgio passed away on July 4, 1925, in much agony. The loss was felt throughout Turin. When his family held the funeral, they were shocked to see thousands of people show up, including many of the poor families he had helped throughout his life.

Shortly after his death, friends and supporters gathered testimonies of his virtuous life. It wasn't long before his cause for canonization officially

"Certainly, at a superficial glance, [Bl. Pier Giorgio] Frassati's lifestyle, that of a modern young man who was full of life, does not present anything out of the ordinary. This, however, is the originality of his virtue, which invites us to reflect upon it and impels us to imitate it. In him faith and daily events are harmoniously fused, so that adherence to the Gospel is translated into loving care for the poor and the needy in a continual crescendo until the very last days of the sickness which led to his death. His love for beauty and art, his passion for sports and mountains, his attention to society's problems did not inhibit his constant relationship with the Absolute. Entirely immersed in the mystery of God and totally dedicated to the constant service of his neighbor: thus we can sum up his earthly life!"

— St. John Paul II, Homily from the Beatification Mass of Pier Giorgio Frassati, 4

opened, a process that required Pier Giorgio's body to be exhumed. According to eyewitnesses, his body was found completely incorrupt. Finally, on May 20, 1990, Pope John Paul II, himself an avid mountain-climber and Pier Giorgio devotee, announced his beatification in front of over 50,000 people.

The announcement confirmed what many already knew, that while Pier Giorgio scaled many mountains throughout his short life, he had also reached the heights of sanctity.

LESSONS FROM BL. PIER GIORGIO FRASSATI

It's hard to narrow down the many lessons Pier Giorgio offers, but perhaps we can settle on three. First, Pier Giorgio embodies authentic Catholic charity, one that is fueled by faith. In Scripture we learn that "faith without works is useless" (James 2:20), but the reverse is true, too. Without a spiritual grounding, charity becomes indistinguishable from mere philanthropy or generic kindness.

The secret to Pier Giorgio's success was that he rooted his service in the Eucharist and prayer. His spiritual life wasn't ancillary to his care for the poor. It formed its beating heart. Like him, we can strengthen our service through consistent prayer and devotion.

Second, we see in Pier Giorgio the crucial role that laity must play in building a just society. He anticipated by several decades the Church's new direction on the role of the laity. Fr. Thomas Rosica deemed him "the first saint to have lived the [Catholic social] encyclical *Rerum Novarum*."[81] As a young man, Pier Giorgio chose not to become a priest or religious because he believed he could more effectively apply his gifts as a layperson. He said, "I want to be able to help my people in every way, and I can do this better as a layman than as a priest because in [Italy], priests do not have as much contact with the people as [elsewhere]."[82] This intuition proved right as he joined student protests, participated in political debates, started a newspaper, and connected with many organizations — actions he probably wouldn't be able to handle as a priest. He also embraced moral positions even when unpopular. This was especially clear in his opposition to Fascism. All of this work Pier Giorgio accomplished as an ordinary layman, exemplifying how any of us, regardless of our state of life, can significantly influence the culture.

Finally, Pier Giorgio demonstrates the need for holistic charity. He knew that true charity required serving the whole person, not just their material needs. Pier Giorgio's niece once observed, "He would do everything for those [poor] families — carry them coal on his back, find the men jobs, buy them shoes. Above all he gave them himself."[83] Pier Giorgio preferred not to delegate his responsibilities to others and he never simply passed out money without interacting. Instead, he gave poor friends his entire care, attention, and devotion — he gave himself.

Reflecting on this mode of service, Pier Giorgio said, "I prefer to deliver the packages personally, because that way I can also encourage the people a bit, give them hope that their lives will change, and above all I can convince them to offer their sufferings to God and to go to Mass."[84] Following his lead, we can offer people in need our whole being, in addition to money, food, and clothing. A nice compliment, a couple hours of listening, or a few words of spiritual encouragement are all ways to give not just handouts, but personal care.

CHAPTER 8

ST. VINCENT DE PAUL

In my early twenties, around the time I became Catholic, I stumbled across a line from a book by Evangelical author Shane Claiborne that would change my life forever: "The great tragedy in the church," he said, "is not that rich Christians do not *care* about the poor but that rich Christians do not *know* the poor. When the worlds of poverty and wealth collide, the resulting powerful fusion can change the world."[85]

For years I had considered myself a pretty charitable guy. I gave to my local church each week. I contributed monthly to a world relief organization. Every now and then I'd give a few bucks to a beggar on the side of the road. But that line pierced me like a sword. It convicted me that while I helped the poor and vulnerable from a distance, I didn't actually *know* any marginalized people. Most of my friends lived just like me: solidly middle-class lives, never worrying about food, shelter, or work. My charity was impersonal and involved no direct encounter.

But reading that challenging line had a transformative effect. I began seeking to meet and befriend people in need. One day, I encountered a few homeless men living in the woods. We shared laughs and food. Then I took them to a barber, where they taught me the tremendous dignity a new haircut imparts (something I always took for granted). Another time I sauntered through the poorest section of Orlando exchanging smiles and conversations with whomever I happened to meet. The people I encountered were short on money, but high on joy and faith. I learned why Jesus said, "Blessed are the poor."

Through intentional acts like these I sampled that "powerful fusion" that can change the world. It wasn't until several years later, though, that I discovered a man whose entire life testified to that nuclear force.

Vincent de Paul was born in southwest France in 1581. His parents were not wealthy, which meant as a boy he spent much of his time working the fields and tending the pigs. Yet he showed an early talent for reading and writing, so at age 14 his parents sent him to college to study for the priesthood.

Vincent excelled at school. After just one year, he was invited to join the Franciscans. He received his minor orders and his tonsure, the typical Franciscan haircut, and spent the next seven years studying theology. In an unusual move, he was ordained on September 23, 1600, at the young age of twenty.

But after a few blissful years as a young priest, tragedy struck in a most unexpected way. In July 1605, Vincent received news that an old friend had died, leaving Vincent a considerable sum of money. Vincent sailed out to Marseilles to collect it. However, on the voyage back, his small ship was attacked by pirates. Vincent later recounted that three large ships full of Muslim pirates bore down and opened fire. They killed three passengers and injured most others — including Vincent, who took an arrow to the arm. The pirates then boarded the ship, took the passengers captive, and transferred them to Tunisia. After parading the prisoners through town, they then sold them as slaves, with Vincent spending two hard years in bondage.

> "If you help the poor and the needy, God will always provide you with the help you need."
>
> — St. Vincent de Paul[86]

A WHIRLING TURN OF EVENTS

Vincent worked under a tough master, a former Christian who had converted to Islam and had taken three wives. One of those wives, a Turkish woman, often wandered the fields and soon befriended Vincent. One day, she became struck by Vincent's kindness and upbeat attitude. She was even more surprised to discover he was a Catholic priest. Something drew her toward the faith he spoke of. So she ran home, reproached her husband, and begged him to return to Christ. Her husband responded to her pleas, repented, and decided to not only free Vincent, but personally help him flee northern Africa. The two crunched into a small rowing boat and amazingly crossed the Mediterranean Sea in the vessel, avoiding pirates and arriving safely back in France on April 28, 1607. After two years of slavery, Vincent was now a free man.

I can't imagine such a whirling turn of events, from grueling bondage to an adventurous sea voyage. Some critics dismiss the whole episode as legendary, but there's really no good explanation as to why it would be invented, presumably by Vincent — his letters in which it appears are universally accepted as authentic.

Upon landing back in France, the two men went their separate ways. The former slave-master entered a monastery, and Vincent began serving in local parishes and abbeys. Yet he couldn't stay hidden for long. Word spread about his remarkable virtue and wisdom, and one day he received a surprising invitation to serve as the Queen's personal chaplain. Vincent accepted and at first enjoyed the post, which came with all the food, riches, and ease he could ever ask for. But he eventually sensed God calling him elsewhere. He yearned to move beyond the worldly comforts of the palace to plant his life alongside the lost and forgotten. He chose to make an option for the poor and vulnerable.

LIVING THE GOSPEL, LOVING THE POOR

"As far as the social justice question goes, I don't think you can be an evangelist, or part of this evangelical movement in the church, without being as clearly committed to social justice as the church has been in the past. We can't preach the Gospel and not live it.

"If we don't love the poor, and do all we can to improve their lot, we're going to go to Hell. It's very clear from the gospels that we have the duty to do that."

— Archbishop Charles Chaput, O.F.M. Cap.[87]

But Vincent realized that probably the best way for him to serve the poor would be to leverage his powerful connections. So in 1613, Vincent accepted a position assisting the wealthy and influential Gondi family, whom he met while serving the Queen. The Gondis asked Vincent to tutor their children. What excited him most, though, was their additional request to serve as chaplain to the many peasants working on their estates. While helping the poor laborers, Vincent really came alive. They affirmed his calling to serve the vulnerable and alleviate their sufferings. He again decided to dedicate his whole life to that sort of work.

In 1617, Vincent returned to the parish priesthood. Only a few months into his pastorate, he learned of a family in his parish facing great distress. They had little money, almost no food, and worst of all, each member of the family had fallen ill. So Vincent appealed to his parishioners, and they responded immediately. Money, food, and help generously poured in until they met all the family's needs. But Vincent realized that within a couple weeks the help would subside and the family would be saddled again with the same problems.

That's when he had an idea: if he could organize a community of caring and committed parishioners, who could take turns caring for needy families, visiting them on a regular basis, they could provide a more permanent and personal form of service.

So on August 20, 1617, he formed his first charitable group, which consisted entirely of women. They called themselves the "Servants of the Poor" (later the "Ladies of Charity"). And, after they served many parish families through this personal form of charity, Vincent soon expanded their mission. Within a few years he had them launching missionary projects, starting new hospitals, gathering relief funds to help war victims, and ransoming slaves from North Africa. Vincent even developed a Rule for the group, weaving into it the core tenants of his spirituality: seeing Christ in the poor and serving the poor through personal charity. The women inspired other communities, too. Soon dozens of similar groups flourished around France.

BL. FRÉDÉRIC OZANAM

Inspired by Vincent de Paul's example, twenty-year-old Bl. Frederic Ozanam (1813–1853) co-founded the St. Vincent de Paul Society in 1833. Present now in thousands of Catholic parishes around the world, the society serves poor people through hands-on charity, requiring its members to visit the poor in person.

As Bl. Frederic explained, visiting and personally encouraging the poor paves the way for a mutually beneficial relationship:

"We should care for the poor in a way that honors them, so that they can reciprocate our gifts.

"Help is humiliating when it appeals to men from below, taking heed only of their material wants. It humiliates when there is no reciprocity. When you give a poor man nothing but bread or clothes, there is no likelihood of his ever giving you anything in return.

"But help honors when it appeals to him from above. It respects him when it deals with his soul, with his religious, moral, and political education, and with all that emancipates him from his passions. Help honors when, to the bread that nourishes, it adds the visit that consoles, advice that enlightens, the friendly handshake that lifts up flagging courage. It esteems the poor man when it treats him with respect, not only as an equal, but as a superior, since he is suffering what perhaps we are incapable of suffering. After all, he is the messenger of God to us, sent to prove our justice and our charity, and to save us by our works.

"Help then becomes honorable, because it may become mutual. Every person who gives a kind word, good advice, a consolation today, may tomorrow need a kind word, advice, or consolation. The hand that you clasp clasps yours in return. That indigent family whom you love loves you in return, and will have largely acquitted themselves toward you when they shall have prayed for you."[88]

One of the more famous groups sparked by the Servants of the Poor was the "Daughters of Charity." In 1633, along with the aristocratic widow, and eventual saint, Louise de Marillac, Vincent persuaded noble and wealthy Parisian women to band together, collect funds, and assist the poor in practical ways. He even envisioned them becoming a new religious order, but one of a different kind. He didn't want these new sisters to be enclosed in cloisters. In his day, all women religious lived, worked, and prayed within a convent, rarely venturing beyond its walls. But Vincent believed this constricted their charity. Seeing the deep congruence between the corporal and spiritual works of mercy, he noted: "When you leave your prayer to care for a sick person, you leave God for God: to care for a sick person is to pray."[89]

Like St. Frances of Rome before him, he enjoined the Daughters to make the whole world their convent:

"For a monastery you have the homes of the sick and that of your superior; for your cell, a rented room; for your chapel, the parish church; for a cloister, the streets of the city; for enclosure, obedience…. Fear of God is your grill, and modesty your veil."[90]

After forming many communities of women, he launched a new community of priests called the Congregation of the Mission. The members lived a common life, eschewed ecclesiastical positions, preached throughout the countryside, and especially served convicts in prison and peasants in the fields. The community was so successful that the archbishop of Paris asked Vincent to train the diocesan seminarians.

Vincent's fame continued to spread. Requests poured in from overseas to evangelize slaves and prisoners, and work with poor laborers. To the worldly excesses of seventeenth-century France, Vincent presented a much-needed example of selfless charity, and his disciples carried that model into the world. One scene illustrates Vincent's high reputation. Lying on his deathbed, King Louis XIII requested that Vincent come visit him. When Vincent arrived, the King said, "Oh, Monsieur Vincent! If I am restored to health I shall appoint no bishops unless they have spent three years with you."[91]

DIAMONDS ONLY FOR THE RICH?

A wealthy woman once visited the twentieth-century activist Dorothy Day and pulled a large diamond ring off her finger. She handed it to Dorothy and asked her to use it for good. Dorothy dropped it into her pocket.

Later that day, a homeless woman knocked on the door at Dorothy's Catholic Worker house, begging for money. Dorothy calmly reached into her pocket and gave her the diamond ring.

Dorothy's friends were appalled. Later, while alone, they asked Dorothy if it would not have been better to sell the ring and use the money to rent a room for the beggar woman. Or perhaps they could have invested the money in a bank for her.

Dorothy replied, "She can do that with the ring if she wants to. She can sell it and go on a vacation if she wants, or she can just wear it on her finger and enjoy it if that's what she wants. Do you think God created diamonds only for the rich?"[92]

Dorothy's response exhibits not just one, but two key principles of Catholic social teaching. Not only did she lavishly take an option for the poor by gifting the diamond ring, she also embraced the principle of subsidiarity, which says that decisions should be made at the lowest level possible. In this case, the lady receiving the ring should decide how to use it — not Dorothy, not her friends, and not the state.

A MULTIFACETED OPTION FOR THE POOR

Vincent had a special love for orphans and handicapped children, some of society's most vulnerable people. In his day, as in ours, some families actually deformed their children on purpose to elicit more pity and handouts. It was also common for parents to dump handicapped children off at a municipal asylum where they were typically ill-treated or allowed to die of hunger.

This appalled Vincent and his wealthy sisters, who decided to literally "make an option," or a choice, for these forgotten children. They began with twelve randomly chosen boys and girls, whom they offered to raise and care for. Later, the Ladies of Charity moved into a special house for the children that included four nurses. Over the next three years they welcomed more than 4,000 boys and girls.

Following this success, Vincent turned his attention to another forgotten group: the disabled homeless. In what some consider "one of the greatest works of charity of the seventeenth century,"[93] Vincent established a new asylum, which over the years sheltered 40,000 poor people. Unlike other shelters of the day, Vincent's offered residents the chance to perform useful work in addition to meeting their material needs — affirming another Catholic social principle, the dignity of work and the rights of workers.

These examples demonstrate Vincent's multifaceted approach to serving the poor. He addressed institutional dysfunction by setting up hospitals, building asylums, and softening the hearts of the aristocracy. But he also addressed on-the-ground problems and had no problem getting his hands dirty. For example, when poor people died and had no family to care for them, Vincent personally dug their graves. He swept the streets and town squares to get rid of excessive dirt, which was a main carrier of the plague. Perhaps most remarkably, Vincent's soup kitchens served more than 15,000 people each day — and he was often seen serving alongside the other volunteers, greeting each visitor with a smile.[94]

Vincent was especially passionate about helping the poor slaves of North Africa. Having shared their lot for two years, he commiserated with their struggles. Roughly 25,000 prisoners lived in bondage, most of them Christian and most carried away from their families by Turkish pirates. Their captors treated them like animals, forcing them to endure beastly labor without any bodily or spiritual care.

In response, Vincent worked tirelessly both to ease their burdens and to help free them. He regularly sent missionaries to the slaves to offer teaching and the sacraments. He personally connected with the slave's families to facilitate secret messages back and forth. He and the Daughters of Charity also collected ransom money and, by the time of his death, were able to free over 1,200 slaves.[95]

WORKS OF MERCY

Dorothy Day once claimed that "everything a baptized person does each day should be directly or indirectly related to the corporal and spiritual works of mercy." The works of mercy refer to fourteen specific acts of compassion that offer concrete ways to live out the option for the poor and vulnerable. They're traditionally grouped into two categories.

The corporal works, so named because they involve the body, include:

The spiritual works of mercy include:

- Feeding the hungry
- Giving drink to the thirsty
- Clothing the naked
- Sheltering the homeless
- Visiting the sick
- Freeing the captive
- Burying the dead

- Instructing the ignorant
- Counseling the doubtful
- Admonishing sinners
- Bearing wrongs patiently
- Forgiving offenses willingly
- Comforting the afflicted
- Praying for the living and the dead

Following Dorothy's adage, we might consider starting each morning by reflecting on ways we can carry out specific works of mercy that day.

THE BEST FRIEND OF THE POOR

In 1656, Vincent acquired a fever he could not shake off. He developed strong pains and then ulcers in his legs, which made him unable to walk. The ulcers worsened for the next few years until Vincent finally died, sitting in his chair, on September 27, 1660. The bishop who celebrated Vincent's funeral said during his homily that even though Vincent came from the country, he was far from a "simple rustic." During his lifetime he had "changed the face of the Church."[96] Another biographer said it more poignantly: "When Vincent died, the poor of Paris lost their best friend."[97]

Local devotion grew quickly. Vincent was beatified one year after his death and canonized four years later. Then in 1885, Pope Leo XIII named him the universal patron of all works of charity.

Centuries later, Vincent's legacy continues on. It's seen through the practical charity of the St. Vincent de Paul Society, which is active in thousands of parishes. And it's evident in two worldwide orders, the Vincentians (Congregation of the Mission) and the Daughters of Charity, also known as the Sisters of Charity of Saint Vincent de Paul.

LESSONS FROM ST. VINCENT DE PAUL

When studying St. Vincent's life we find a nearly endless supply of inspiration — and astonishment. To accomplish all that he did, it seems each of his days must have lasted a hundred hours. But among the many lessons we can glean, three stand out.

First, Vincent shows the most effective form of charity is personal. This was arguably his most important and lasting message. From his early parish communities, to his ministry to the slaves, to the Society he inspired, Vincent reinforced that "powerful fusion" in which the worlds of poverty and wealth collide. He knew that the closer we are to someone, the better we can serve their needs. This is true for our friends and family members and it's equally true for the poor and vulnerable.

> "It is not sufficient for me to love God if I do not love my neighbor. I belong to God and to the poor."
>
> — St. Vincent de Paul[98]

But Vincent's lesson isn't only that personal relationships help us serve the poor. They also transforms us. From the poor we learn the value of simplicity and the witness of unshakable faith. We encounter Christ himself, who identifies with those on the margins. Befriending the poor is thus beneficial to everyone.

Secondly, Vincent teaches us that an "option for the poor" involves not just helping the poor, but inspiring *others* to help the poor, too. Throughout his life, Vincent leveraged his influence and relationships to help the rich and comfortable give their lives in service. He knew that, by himself, he could never feed thousands of people or liberate hundreds of African slaves. But with the help of generous donors and friends, he could achieve remarkable feats.

The option for the poor and vulnerable is not an individual pursuit. It's a communal mission, and the more we enable each other to serve, the more impact we'll have.

Finally, Vincent's work demonstrates how the "option for the poor" operates on many different levels. Vincent addressed the institutional causes of poverty by fighting against slavery and helping the jobless find work. But he also met people's immediate needs like food and shelter. Catholic social teaching maintains that countering poverty involves both justice and charity, institutional reform and personal compassion. Vincent provides an excellent model of this two-pronged approach.

THE DIGNITY OF WORK AND THE RIGHTS OF WORKERS

The economy must serve people, not the other way around. **Work is more than a way to make a living; it is a form of continuing participation in God's creation.** If the dignity of work is to be protected, then the basic rights of workers must be respected — the right to productive work, to decent and fair wages, to the organization and joining of unions, to private property, and to economic initiative.[99]

CHAPTER 9

ST. BENEDICT
OF NURSIA

Although we remember St. Benedict of Nursia as the founding patriarch of Western monasticism, we don't have much background on him. Most of what we know comes from the *Dialogues* of Pope St. Gregory the Great, written in the sixth century, a few decades after Benedict's death.

According to Pope Gregory, Benedict was born around the year 480 in the small Italian province of Nursia. He and his twin sister, Scholastica, experienced a privileged upbringing. They were raised in comfort and high culture, and during his boyhood Benedict's parents sent him off to Rome to study the liberal arts.

However, the city's squalor and depravity revolted the young boy. He encountered priests living worldly lives, devoted to pleasure and vice, and heard serious heresies preached from their pulpits. Desiring to live a more noble life, the boy fled south to the hills of Subiaco. He left behind a promising future in Rome, but he considered that a small price to pay for a life united to God.

On the way to Subiaco, he encountered an elderly monk named Romanus, who asked him where he was going. Benedict revealed his plan to live the life of a hermit and begged Romanus not to share his secret. The monk agreed, but requested that Benedict allow him to check on him every now and then.

Benedict found his new hermitage in a secluded cave, near the ruins of one of Nero's palaces, in which he lived alone for three years. Day and night he prayed to God. He mastered his earthly passions through fasting and discipline, and his only human interaction occurred with Romanus. The two never met face-to-face, though, after their initial encounter. Benedict's cave was located on a steep impasse, so when Romanus visited, he had to lower food into the cave from a high, overhanging rock. Romanus usually tied bread to a long rope with a little bell on the end. When Benedict heard the ring, he rushed over, untied the bread, and gave the rope an extra tug as a sign of thanks.

However, one year during Holy Week the bell stopped ringing. Benedict remained calm. Alone in the wilderness, he wasn't sure where he would find any food, but he knew that God would provide.

And sure enough, as if on cue, a strange priest appeared at the mouth of the cave. He was the first person Benedict had seen in years. Walking in, the man spoke: "Rise up, brother, and let us dine, because today is the feast of Easter."[100] Benedict rose and ate a sumptuous meal with the priest. Afterward, the two men prayed together and the priest departed in peace.

It wasn't long before the saintly hermit's reputation spread to nearby communities. Townspeople flocked to Benedict's cave to hear his soothing voice and learn from his extraordinary virtue. As Pope Pius XII beautifully remarked:

"Indeed that bright light that shone from the dark cave of Subiaco spread so far and wide that it even reached ... nobles and devout persons of the city of Rome [who] began to resort to him and commended their children to be brought up by him in the service of Almighty God."[101]

Monks from a nearby monastery visited Benedict and begged him to serve as their abbot, their previous leader having passed away. Benedict reluctantly agreed. However, he regretted the decision almost immediately. He found the monks unruly and undisciplined. They didn't work, and their prayer life was lax. For their part, the monks chafed against Benedict's rigorous habits. They eventually decided to poison him. But Benedict recognized their plan and avoided the attempt. After making the sign of the cross over the monks, he said, "God forgive you, brothers. Why have you plotted this wicked thing against me? Did I not tell you beforehand that my ways would not accord with yours? Go and find an abbot to your taste, for after what you have done you can no longer keep me with you."[102]

He wished them well and returned to his cave at Subiaco. And for the moment, it seemed the famous monk of Subiaco would forever remain in his cave.

MONASTIC LIFE

Soon, however, new groups of monks discovered the holy hermit. Like those before, they begged Benedict to lead them. And their requests eventually convinced Benedict to accept. But this time the experience began far more positively.

Benedict instituted a monastery of twelve communities, each with twelve monks. His sanctity deeply impacted the men around him. The monastery grew as Benedict became known as a wonder-worker, performing miracles and raising people from the dead. Scores of new followers flocked to the Subiaco monastery.

However, Benedict also aroused jealousy and persecution, which inevitably arrive with great fame. A neighboring priest tried to sabotage Benedict's work — first by slandering him and then by poisoning him. To spare his followers this tension, Benedict decided to leave Subiaco.

After a somber farewell, he gathered a handful of monks and journeyed to the town of Cassino. The town, perched on a high mountain near Naples, had been destroyed by Goths, and the people, though formerly Christian, had relapsed into paganism. They worshiped at a temple dedicated to Apollo and offered sacrifices in a nearby forest. Their idolatry scandalized Benedict, and he decided that his first work, after a forty-day fast, was to win the people back to the faith. After he converted them, he smashed all their idols, overthrew the altar, burned the groves, and in place of the pagan temple built a chapel dedicated to St. John the Baptist.[103]

In the year 520, Benedict consecrated the mountain to God, inaugurating a new monastery on the ashes of the pagan temple. The monastery, which he called Monte Cassino, quickly gained attention for its impressive virtue, sanctity, and hospitality.

A MEANS OF SANCTIFICATION

"*Human work* proceeds directly from persons created in the image of God and called to prolong the work of creation by subduing the earth, both with and for one another. Hence work is a duty: "If anyone will not work, let him not eat" (Gen 3:14–19). Work honors the Creator's gifts and the talents received from him. It can also be redemptive. By enduring the hardship of work in union with Jesus, the carpenter of Nazareth and the one crucified on Calvary, man collaborates in a certain fashion with the Son of God in his redemptive work. He shows himself to be a disciple of Christ by carrying the cross, daily, in the work he is called to accomplish. Work can be a means of sanctification and a way of animating earthly realities with the Spirit of Christ."

— *Catechism of the Catholic Church,* 2427

"[T]he holy monastery built there was a haven and shelter of highest learning and of all the virtues, and in those very troubled times was, as it were, a pillar of the Church and a bulwark of the faith."[104]

Benedict and his monks flourished for decades at Monte Cassino. But the famous monastery wasn't Benedict's only legacy. His greater and more timeless impact came through his revolutionary Rule.

WORKING FOR GOD'S GLORY

Brother Lawrence lived in a Carmelite monastery in the seventeenth century, but unlike St. Benedict and friends, he was not a monk. Lawrence served as a simple layman, eager to help his community by sweeping, cooking, and cleaning. While he joined in some of their religious activities, he kept mostly to himself and often slipped by unnoticed.

Today, however, Brother Lawrence is remembered as one of the most noted and beloved spiritual authors. His short classic, *The Practice the Presence of God*, contains practical advice on cultivating spiritual depth in the ordinary world. The book aims to help normal men and women converse daily with the Lord — to sanctify their work by doing it for the glory of God.

"Our sanctification [does] not depend upon changing our works," Lawrence wrote, "but in doing that for God's sake which we commonly do for our own."[105]

Lawrence realized that we sanctify our work by offering it to God. And because we can do this with *any* sort of work, no task is off limits. He said: "We ought not to be weary of doing little things for the love of God, who regards not the greatness of the work, but the love with which it is performed."[106]

BENEDICT'S 'RULE'

Drawing on earlier monastic writings, Benedict's Rule laid out the principles of Christian community life. The Rule is not a spiritual treatise. It reads more like a law book than a prayer guide. Also, some of the sections apply only to monks, such as the advice on the proper qualities of an abbot or the liturgical norms for the monastery.

But all men and women can benefit from the Rule's wisdom regarding everyday activities. For Benedict, the spiritual life was rooted in the ordinary. He believed the path to God lay in the mundane, routine actions of life — not in grand miracles or spiritual ecstasy. And this is why he placed such a strong emphasis on work.

Chapter 48 contains the Rule's main section on work, and begins with one of Benedict's most famous adages:

"Idleness is the enemy of the soul. Therefore, the brothers should have specified periods for manual labor.… When they live by the labor of their hands, as our fathers and the apostles did, then they are really monks."[107]

Part of this labor includes cooking, which the Rule expects all able monks to help with. "By mutually serving each other," the Rule notes, "they will acquire a large increase of charity and merit."[108]

Yet Benedict discourages *vain* work. From a spiritual perspective, the purpose of labor is not to show off or only to make lots of money. It's to serve the community and grow closer to God:

"If there be any artisans in the monastery, let them exercise their respective crafts, with all humility and reverence.… Should any of them get proud from the notion that he is benefiting the monastery by [his work], let him be instantly put away from his trade, and prohibited to exercise it any more, unless the Abbot, seeing him humble, should command him to resume it."[109]

In other parts of the Rule, Benedict lays out a rather precise schedule that includes time every day for manual labor. Yet he leaves room for those unable to carry out the more grueling tasks. He specifies that: "Brothers who are sick or weak should be given a type of work or craft that will keep them busy without overwhelming them or driving them away. The abbot must take their infirmities into account."[110]

Equal parts practical and sensitive, the Rule positions work, alongside prayer and study, as a foundation of a well-grounded life.

ST. JOSEPH THE WORKER

Scripture doesn't tell us much about St. Joseph, but it does highlight his occupation as a carpenter. Joseph was a "blue-collar," hardworking laborer — a "just man," according to Matthew's gospel — who literally served the Lord through his work. We know he passed this work on to his son, who practiced carpentry for many of the first thirty years of his life.

In 1955, Pope Pius XII designated May 1 as the Feast of St. Joseph the Worker. The announcement was not well-received by communist leaders, who saw it as an affront to their materialistic views of work. But regardless of his political purpose, the pope's aim was to provide a new significance and spiritual value to work. The opening prayer of the liturgy for this feast day begins:

"O God, Creator of all things, who laid down for the human race the law of work, graciously grant that by the example of Saint Joseph and under his patronage we may complete the works you set us to do and attain the rewards you promise. Through our Lord Jesus Christ, your Son, who lives and reigns with you in the unity of the Holy Spirit, one God, forever and ever."[111]

ORA ET LABORA

In Benedict's day, most people viewed labor as degrading and servile. For centuries the Romans had turned conquered people into slaves, forcing them to perform menial tasks and difficult work. Yet through his Rule and example, Benedict introduced the novel idea that labor was not only dignified and honorable, but also a path to holiness. Thus the Benedictine tradition developed the motto *ora et labora*, meaning "pray and work."

One story illustrates this point. Pope Gregory tells of a rough young man who came to join Benedict's monastery. Benedict, happy to receive him, clothed the young man in the monastic habit and, noting his well-built frame, assigned him to clear the underbrush around a nearby lake. The man happily agreed. Using an axe, he slashed at the weeds and bushes, making space for a new garden. But during one particular swing, as he lifted the axe high into the air, the axe head flew off the handle. It landed with a splash in the middle of the lake and sank to the bottom. The dejected man rushed back to Benedict, worried that the abbot would chide him.

But he couldn't have expected what happened next. The gracious Benedict led him back to the water's edge, then asked for the axe shaft. Upon receiving it, he said a prayer and dipped it into the lake. Immediately the iron head rose to the surface. It then slowly floated back to the shore and leapt up into the air, attaching itself onto the shaft.

Benedict handed the axe back to the stunned man, saying in a kind voice: "Take your tool; work and be comforted."[112]

Benedict performed many other miracles that affirmed the value of work. One day, his monks complained about a large stone they needed to move in order to build a new block of cells in their monastery. Even when several monks combined their strength, they couldn't move it. But Benedict visited the stone, prayed over it and gave it his blessing, then suggested the monks try again. This time they lifted and moved it as if it was made of feathers. Symbolically, their work opened a new space for prayer — the perfect image of *ora et labora*.

In 543, more than twenty years after building Monte Cassino, Benedict predicted his time had come to an end. After digging his own grave — one final affirmation of hard work — he visited his sister, Scholastica, who by that time had developed her own reputation as a holy nun.

Benedict finally died on March 21, 543. At the time of his death, his Rule was followed only in a few monasteries and convents. But by the seventh and eighth centuries, his Rule had spread far and wide. Pope Pius XII noted the significance:

"During a dark and turbulent age, when agriculture [and] honorable craft ... were little esteemed and shamefully neglected by nearly all, there arose in Benedictine monasteries an almost countless multitude of farmers, craftsmen, and learned people.... From renascent barbarism, from destruction and ruin, they happily led them back to ... patient labor, to the light of truth, to a civilization renewed in wisdom and charity."[113]

When the emperor Charlemagne (742–814) and his son, Louis the Pious (778–840), embarked on a reform of monasticism, they chose Benedict's Rule as the most suitable model. Louis imposed it on all monasteries throughout Western Europe. Today, thousands of people pray and work in the Benedictine tradition, seeing their work as an effective path to God.

ST. JOSEMARÍA AND THE SPIRITUALITY OF WORK

One saint known for his spirituality of work was St. Josemaría Escrivá, the twentieth-century founder of Opus Dei. Throughout his many writings he encouraged Christians to find dignity and purpose in their labor, for like St. Benedict he rejected the idea that work was pointless toil. Instead, he maintained, if understood properly work could become an avenue to sanctity. In the few excerpts below we see echoes of St. Benedict's famous model, *ora et labora*:

"Professional work, whatever it is, becomes a lamp to enlighten your colleagues and friends. That is why I usually tell [people]: 'What use is it telling me that so and so is a good son of mine — a good Christian — but a bad shoemaker?' If he doesn't try to learn his trade well, or doesn't give his full attention to it, he won't be able to sanctify it or offer it to Our Lord. The sanctification of ordinary work is, as it were, the hinge of true spirituality for people who, like us, have decided to come close to God while being at the same time fully involved in temporal affairs."[114]

"Persevere in the exact fulfillment of the obligations of the moment. That work — humble, monotonous, small — is prayer expressed in action that prepares you to receive the grace of the other work — great and wide and deep — of which you dream."[115]

"It is time for us Christians to shout from the rooftops that work is a gift from God and that it makes no sense to classify men differently, according to their occupation, as if some jobs were nobler than others. Work, all work, bears witness to the dignity of man, to his dominion over creation."[116]

LESSONS FROM ST. BENEDICT OF NURSIA

Through both his life and his Rule, St. Benedict offers many lessons on prayer, community, and the monastic life. But he also has much to teach us about work.

First, Benedict reveals that by working we participate in God's own life. Through small acts of sub-creation — cooking food, drafting reports, building new structures — we can in a small way share in God's creative power. By seeing our work not as pointless repetition but as a chance to co-create with God, we charge it with new dignity.

In addition, hard work unites us closer to God's Incarnate Son. As Pope Pius XII observed, "Even Jesus, as a youth, still sheltered within the domestic walls, did not disdain to ply the carpenter's trade in his foster father's workshop; He wished to consecrate human toil with divine sweat."[117] Christ worked hard, in relative obscurity, for many years before beginning his public ministry. Therefore whenever we face stressful or challenging situations in our jobs, we can bring those difficulties to Him in prayer, confident that he can relate. "Come to me," Jesus invites, "all you who labor and are burdened, and I will give you rest" (Mt 11:28).

Second, Benedict's Rule shows how work dignifies our role in society. While it's true our identity is not rooted in what we do, it's also true that through labor we are able to serve our community. Many people feel empty when they're able to work but unable to find a job. This is because work imparts value and dignity. Pope Francis echoed this point during his homily on Labor Day 2013:

"Work gives us dignity! Those who work have dignity, a special dignity, a personal dignity: men and women who work are dignified. Instead, those who do not work do not have this dignity. But there are many who want to work and cannot. This is a burden on our conscience, because when society is organized in such a way that not everyone has the opportunity to work, to be anointed with the dignity of work, then there is something wrong with that society: it is not right! It goes against God himself, who wanted our dignity, starting from here."[118]

Finally, Benedict teaches us that the fruit of work is not only what it produces in the *world*, but what it produces within *us*. As most of us know from experience, hard works tends to clear our mind, direct our attention, and, sometimes, facilitate our prayer. Ordinary work, such as washing the dishes or tending the garden, can take a on a spiritual dimension if done with the right attitude. In his encyclical *Laborem Exercens* ("On Human Work"), Pope John Paul II accentuated this key Benedictine lesson.

"Work," he said, "remains a good thing, not only because it is useful and enjoyable, but also because it expresses and increases the worker's dignity. Through work we not only transform the world, we are transformed ourselves, becoming 'more a human being.'"[119]

Hard work elevates the mind and the spirit, giving it a sense of mastery and accomplishment that spills over into the spiritual life.

CHAPTER 10
SERVANT OF GOD
DOROTHY DAY

"Don't call me a saint," Dorothy Day once quipped, and some are happy to oblige. They wonder why Dorothy's cause for canonization is moving forward — and perhaps why she's featured in this book about saints. After all, how can a spitfire, twentieth-century social activist, who participated in labor strikes, protested war and abortion, went to prison, and complained that the Church wasn't paying enough attention to its own teachings be listed alongside holy mystics and contemplatives?

Even decades after her death Dorothy remains an enigma. We can't easily pigeonhole her, either as an activist, a liberal, a conservative, a Democrat, a Republican, or a libertarian. Those on the political left balk at her condemnation of abortion and contraception and her unwavering devotion to the Church. Those on the right chill at her socialist sympathies, her anti-war stance, and her pre-conversion abortion.

Yet as Cardinal Timothy Dolan announced at the 2012 gathering of bishops, "I am convinced [Dorothy] is a saint for our time. She exemplifies what's best in Catholic life, that ability we have to be 'both-and' not 'either-or.'"[120]

In Dorothy's view, the Church's social teachings form a complete, indivisible package. We have only two choices: either we accept the whole gift or we reject it all. The only thing we can't do is fragment it, taking it piecemeal and dismissing those parts that conflict with our political or social views.

Dorothy's coherent devotion to Catholic social teaching has made her a bridge between different groups in the Church. As Vatican reporter John Allen, Jr., observes, "The church at the grass roots in the United States has been badly splintered into a kind of peace-and-justice crowd on the left and a pro-life crowd on the right. Day is one of those few figures who has traction in both those groups."[121]

Regardless of any controversy surrounding Dorothy's mission, supporters and skeptics agree on at least one thing: Dorothy relentlessly cared for the poor, especially the working poor. Specifically, she championed the rights of workers more vigorously and personally than perhaps any other saint.

FROM *THE JUNGLE* TO PRISON

Dorothy Day was born in 1897, just four years before Bl. Pier Giorgio Frassati. Like Pier Giorgio, she was raised in a non-religious home. But unlike Pier Giorgio, she grew up extremely poor. After losing almost everything in the 1906 San Francisco earthquake, her family moved to Chicago, where they lived in a small tenement flat. Fruit crates served as book cases and nail kegs as kitchen stools. The curtains were sewn together from old clothes.[122] Dorothy's keen understanding of poverty dates from this period, which gave her personal experience of the shame that comes with poverty and joblessness.

During these early years, Dorothy also developed a subtle draw to Christianity. One day, while searching for one of her friends, Dorothy walked in on her friend's mother, Mrs. Barrett, who was praying on her knees at the side of her bed. Without embarrassment, Mrs. Barrett looked up, greeted Dorothy, and explained where her daughter was. Then she went back to praying. The

---

THE RIGHT TO PRODUCTIVE WORK

"Work is for man, not man for work. Everyone should be able to draw from work the means of providing for his life and that of his family, and of serving the human community....

"Access to employment and to professions must be open to all without unjust discrimination: men and women, healthy and disabled, natives and immigrants. For its part society should, according to circumstances, help citizens find work and employment....

"A *just wage* is the legitimate fruit of work. To refuse or withhold it can be a grave injustice. In determining fair pay both the needs and the contributions of each person must be taken into account."

— *Catechism of the Catholic Church*, 2428–2434

seemingly insignificant encounter played a major role in Dorothy's later conversion to Catholicism. As she wrote in her autobiography, *The Long Loneliness*: "I felt a burst of love toward Mrs. Barrett that I have never forgotten, a feeling of gratitude and happiness that warmed my heart."[123]

Dorothy's family slowly recovered in Chicago. When Dorothy was 15, her father found a job as a sports editor, which allowed the family to move to a nicer part of the city. She was proud of their new home. It was larger and more comfortable. It also featured an expansive library where Dorothy fell in love with novelists like Victor Hugo and Charles Dickens.

The most influential book of her youth, however, was Upton Sinclair's *The Jungle*. Set in the slaughterhouses and shipyards of her own Chicago, the book features a Lithuanian immigrant who fights against the filth and violence of the meat industry. The story's powerful call for justice and workers' rights inspired Dorothy. She felt drawn to take long walks in Chicago's South Side, through many neighborhoods mentioned in the novel.

It was during one of these somber pilgrimages that Dorothy realized her life's calling. Walking the streets, and pondering the poor, she sensed a desire to live alongside them: "From that time on my life was to be linked to theirs, their interests would be mine: I had received a call, a vocation, a direction in life."[124]

She carried that calling with her to college. At age 16, Dorothy received a scholarship to attend the University of Illinois at Urbana. There she studied for two years, supporting herself through odd jobs like washing, ironing, and caring for children. She enjoyed the manual labor because it brought her close to the working poor.

While in college, she also developed two great passions: writing and social justice. Dorothy envisioned walking in the footsteps of Upton Sinclair, using her pen to expose and correct gross injustices.

By age 18, however, the restless radical decided she was tired of school. Without a journalism degree, or any real job connection, Dorothy moved to New York City where, unsurprisingly, she had difficulty finding work. None of the city's mainstream newspapers expressed interest in her. Her only job offer came from *The Call*, New York's socialist newsweekly. It paid $5 a week — barely enough to live on — but Dorothy saw it as an invaluable chance to move from reading and dreaming about social change to directly influencing it.

She took the job and began covering rallies, demonstrations, and workers' strikes. And soon she began participating. In November 1917, she went to prison after picketing in front of the White House for women's right to vote. The prison guards treated Dorothy and her companions harshly, which led the prisoners to conduct a hunger strike. Eventually they were freed by a direct order from the president, but the prison stay would not be Dorothy's last.

FROM ALCOHOLIC TO CHAMPION OF WORKERS' RIGHTS

Matt Talbot was born in Dublin, Ireland, in 1856, the second of twelve children. His father and most of his brothers were heavy drinkers. By age 13, he too had become an alcoholic. Almost every day he frequented the pubs, spending all of his money and selling his possessions to buy drinks. But when Matt turned 16, he decided it was time for a change. He pledged to stop drinking, paid off all his debts, began attending daily Mass, and after three months emerged a sober man.

Upon cleaning up his life, Matt channeled his former passions into his work. He took a job at Pembertons, a large building contractor, where his strong work ethic drew admiration from his peers. They noticed how he took on the meanest and hardest jobs and seemed to be a natural-born leader.

In 1911, Matt joined the laborers branch of the Irish Transport and General Workers Union — just two years before Dublin experienced the most devastating labor dispute in its history. Approximately 20,000 workers went on strike, clamoring for living wages and the ability to form unions. Matt joined his fellow laborers and stood up for their rights.

After a year of difficult negotiations, the strike ended peacefully in 1914. Leaders hailed Matt for his leadership and offered special "strike pay." But he refused it saying that he had not earned it. He asked that it be shared among the other strikers instead.

Matt Talbot died in 1925, and exactly fifty years later Pope Paul VI declared him Venerable. Today, he remains a model both for those seeking sobriety and those championing the rights of workers.

THE CHURCH OF THE POOR

Along with Dorothy's growing activism, she also developed her religious sense. In 1922, she roomed with three young women who regularly went to Mass and prayed each day. Their devotion beguiled Dorothy, who concluded "worship, adoration, thanksgiving, supplication ... [are] the noblest acts of which we are capable in this life."[125]

Over the years, she became more attracted to the Catholic Church, specifically because of its concern for the poor and vulnerable:

"I knew nothing of the social teaching of the Church at that time. I had never heard of the encyclicals. [But] I felt that the Church was the Church of the poor, that St. Patrick's had been built from the pennies of servant girls, that it cared for the emigrant, it established hospitals, orphanages, day nurseries, houses of the Good Shepherd, [and] homes for the aged."[126]

But a great tragedy interrupted her seeking. Dorothy engaged in a cheerless love affair, which resulted in her getting pregnant. Unmarried and scared, she made the horrific choice to abort her child. The decision pained her for the rest of her life. To make matters worse, the surgery damaged Dorothy's womb: "For a long time I had thought I could not bear a child, and the longing in my heart for a baby had been growing. My home, I felt, was not a home without one."[127]

Yet several years later, in 1925, while living with her common-law husband, Dorothy conceived again. She considered it nothing less than miraculous, believing the child was a gift from God. In thanks, she committed that the baby would receive a religious upbringing — even though the child's father was a staunch atheist:

"I did not want my child to flounder as I had often floundered. I wanted to believe, and I wanted my child to believe, and if belonging to a church would give her so inestimable a grace as faith in God, and the companionable love of the Saints, then the thing to do was to have her baptized a Catholic."[128]

Dorothy gave birth to Tamar Theresa on March 3, 1926, and had her baptized in a Catholic church. Later that year, Dorothy followed suit. She had become a Catholic.

THE CATHOLIC WORKER

Dorothy had a difficult time mingling her newfound faith and her radical convictions. Few of her Catholic friends bothered with social justice. "Where were the saints trying to change the social order?" she wondered.[129] And most of her radical friends were atheists.

But on December 8, 1932, as Dorothy covered the communist-inspired "Hunger March" in Washington, D.C., something changed. Protesters lined the streets of Washington carrying signs calling for basic workers' rights — jobs, unemployment insurance, old age pensions, relief for mothers and children, and health care. Dorothy didn't share the marchers' communism, but she admired their courage and solidarity. Deeply convicted, she fled to the unfinished Shrine of the Immaculate Conception and prayed in the crypt: "I offered up a special prayer, a prayer which came with tears and anguish, that some way would open up for me to use what talents I possessed for my fellow workers, for the poor."[130]

Little did she know how quickly she'd receive an answer. The next day, back at her apartment in New York, an elderly French emigrant knocked on her door. Peter Maurin introduced himself and then explained the reason for his visit. He yearned for the transformation of society — one in which "it would be easier to be good" — and he had long been praying for a collaborator. A friend suggested he contact Dorothy, and after reading her work, Peter was convinced she was the answer. The wise and witty vagabond, who drew comparisons to Francis of Assisi, believed Dorothy could be a modern Catherine of Siena, someone who could "move mountains, and have influence on governments, temporal and spiritual."[131] The best way to do this, he suggested, would be to start a newspaper.

After much conversation, Dorothy agreed, seeing Peter as the answer to her prayers as much as she was to his. On May 1, 1933, the two launched *The Catholic Worker*. The paper aimed to put Catholic social teaching in ordinary terms and to promote the transformation of society — especially the sphere of work. What set it apart from other radical papers was that it didn't merely complain about social injustice. It called readers to make a personal response.

Dorothy wrote about the conditions of poor people and especially the conditions of workers and the labor movement, then still struggling for recognition. She sought to explain Catholic social teaching in such a way that it would inspire lay volunteers, clergy, and even bishops.

THE RIGHTS OF POOR WORKERS

"Rights must be religiously respected wherever they exist, and it is the duty of the public authority to prevent and to punish injury, and to protect everyone in the possession of his own. Still, when there is question of defending the rights of individuals, the poor and badly off have a claim to especial consideration.... [W]age-earners, since they mostly belong in the mass of the needy, should be specially cared for and protected."

— **Pope Leo XIII**,
Rerum Novarum, **37**

Dorothy and Peter marketed the paper to working men and women, selling it near factories and bustling town squares for just one penny, the same price it remains today. Within six months they were printing over 100,000 copies.

What started as the effort of a newly converted laywoman and a French radical soon became a movement. The newspaper blossomed into Catholic Worker communities and houses all over the world, which to this day center themselves on hospitality, non-violence, workers' rights, and solidarity with the poor.

WORKER'S RIGHTS AND CEMETERY STRIKE

As *The Catholic Worker* took off, and as the Great Depression put millions of men out of work, Dorothy refocused her attention on the rights of workers. She led boycotts of stores that paid low wages. She was upset that hard-working men couldn't support their families: "Why didn't fathers get money enough to take care of their families so that mothers didn't have to work?"[132] She also urged bosses to treat their workers with dignity and view them not as property but as partners.

Some of her most passionate advocacy emerged in support of workers' unions. Dorothy saw them as the earthly expression of the spiritual unity all men share under God. Unions, like the Church, taught that no real boundaries separate one person from another, and that together people can stand in solidarity for their basic rights.

One episode illustrates her point. The 400-acre Calvary Cemetery in Middle Village, Queens, operated by the Archdiocese of New York, was the largest Catholic cemetery in the city. During the twentieth century alone, more than 1.5 million people were buried there. It was so massive, it required 240 workers to maintain and operate.[133]

The cemetery workers, all unionized and almost all Catholic, operated on a contractual basis. Their current contract was set to expire in December 1948, but they had difficulty negotiating a new one. Under the current version, workers received $59.40 for a six-day, forty-eight hour week. However, the Union, representing the workers, requested the next contract be for a five-day, forty-hour week for the same $59.40 wage. They also asked for overtime pay for working more than eight hours a day and for any Saturday work.

The archdiocese rejected both requests — though they did offer a 2.6% wage increase, equivalent to the rise in cost of living — and thus the cemetery workers voted to strike.

THE RIGHT TO STRIKE

"Recourse to a strike is morally legitimate when it cannot be avoided, or at least when it is necessary to obtain a proportionate benefit. It becomes morally unacceptable when accompanied by violence, or when objectives are included that are not directly linked to working conditions or are contrary to the common good."

— *Catechism of the Catholic Church*, 2435

On January 13, 1949, the workers established a picket line at the cemetery's entrance. Thirty-five burials were scheduled that day, forcing the cemetery to construct temporary graves. Some coffins were left to sit on the soil, waiting for permanent burial. Other nearby workers, sympathetic to the strike, soon joined in. It wasn't long before the number of unburied bodies climbed to over 1,000.

Hostility grew between the Union and the archdiocese. Five weeks into the strike, Cardinal Francis Spellman, the Archbishop of New York, brought in seminarians to serve as makeshift gravediggers, effectively replacing the workers on strike. To his credit, the Cardinal was trying to ensure one of the corporal works of mercy, burying the dead.

But this move angered Dorothy, who had been closely following the strike. She felt sympathetic to the workers' cause, especially their right to form unions and strike when necessary. Some of her Catholic Worker community members had picketed with the workers and Dorothy herself had even been arrested for passing out fliers supporting the strike.

On March 4, 1949, Dorothy wrote an eloquent letter to Cardinal Spellman, begging him to end the strike:

"I'm writing to you, because the strike, though small, is a terribly significant one.... It is not just the issue of wages and hours as I can see from the conversations which our workers have had with the men. It is a question of their dignity as men, their dignity as workers, and the right to have a union of their own, and a right to talk over their grievances.

[They deserve] a wage ... [that] would enable the workers to raise and educate their families of six, seven and eight children; a wage [that] would enable them to buy homes to save for homeownership; to [save] for the education of the children. Certainly the wage which they need in these days of high prices and exorbitant rents is not the wage for which they are working."[134]

A week after Dorothy's letter, the two sides reached a compromise. The workers weren't wholly pleased — they earned a wage increase of 8% but still had to work six days — but at least they could get back to work and begin earning income again.

Dorothy continued protesting for workers' rights throughout her life, in many places and for many causes. In 1973, at age seventy-five, she joined Cesar Chavez and the United Farm Workers in California for her final demonstration. Though the protest was nonviolent, she and other protesters were jailed for ten days, the last of her many prison stays.

Dorothy died on November 29, 1980. Despite the controversy, her life remains a model for those pursuing justice and promoting the rights of workers.

OUR PEBBLE IN THE POND

"By fighting for better conditions, by crying out unceasingly for the rights of the workers, the poor, of the destitute ... we can, to a certain extent, change the world; we can work for the oasis, the little cell of joy and peace in a harried world. We can throw our pebble in the pond and be confident that its ever widening circle will reach around the world."[135]

— Dorothy Day

LESSONS FROM SERVANT OF GOD DOROTHY DAY

Dorothy's life of justice offers many lessons. First, she demonstrates the power of laypeople to stand up for worker's rights. Most of the Church's saints have been priests, nuns, brothers, and bishops. Yet today lay men and women compose over 99.9% of the Church.[136] Dorothy provides a model for this majority of pursuing justice without relying on the Church's institutions. She didn't think those institutions were necessarily bad or misguided, she just understood that, as the Second Vatican Council taught, "It belongs to the laity to seek the kingdom of God by engaging in temporal affairs and directing them according to God's will."[137]

Dorothy knew that laypeople could be far more fluid and effective than large Church institutions in addressing workers' rights, and the same holds true today. The institutional Church promotes justice through its teachings and governance, but it still counts on laypeople to carry them out in their social environments. Laypeople must embody these teachings through concrete, personal action.

Second, Dorothy models how to place our faith above our political views. She's so difficult to pigeonhole because she never identified with any political party. She didn't promote the rights of workers because some political group told her to. She protested, marched, wrote, and spoke out because her *faith* demanded it: "You shall not exploit a poor and needy hired servant" (Dt 24:14). She was not ashamed of seeing the world's problems through a Catholic lens: "If I have achieved anything in my life," she once remarked, "it is because I have not been embarrassed to talk about God."[138]

Finally, like so many other saints, Dorothy understood the power of small actions to produce large change. It may seem insignificant to pass out pamphlets advocating for better working conditions, march with a sign down the street, or write a letter to the local newspaper. But it's through an accumulation of these small acts that Dorothy sparked a movement and changed the world.

SOLIDARITY

We are one human family whatever our national, racial, ethnic, economic, and ideological differences. **We are our brothers' and sisters' keepers, wherever they may be.** Loving our neighbor has global dimensions in a shrinking world. At the core of the virtue of solidarity is the pursuit of justice and peace. Pope Paul VI taught that if you want peace, work for justice. The Gospel calls us to be peacemakers. Our love for all our sisters and brothers demands that we promote peace in a world surrounded by violence and conflict.[139]

CHAPTER 11
ST. JOHN PAUL II

O n May 1, 2011, I stood atop the colonnade surrounding St. Peter's Square and let out a sigh. Gazing down at hundreds of thousands of people who had come to celebrate the beatification of Pope John Paul II, I couldn't help but recall St. Peter's observation, made 2,000 years ago: "Lord, it is good that we are here" (Mt 17:4).

The excited crowds poured in from around the world to witness John Paul II becoming a "Blessed," a major step toward his eventual canonization. And what most struck me was the *universality* of the moment. Looking down at the rich and poor, young and old, seeking and confident, all cheering and singing and roaring together, I saw the Church in a nutshell. There she was, the global Church, gathered by Christ — Catholics and others from every nation united in great solidarity.

It made sense, then, that we were all there to celebrate a man many consider "The Solidarity Pope," who in his long life and pontificate lived out the unity that was displayed that day.

LOLEK AND THE UNDERGROUND SEMINARY

Karol Joseph Wojtyla (pronounced "Voy-tee-wa") was born in Poland on May 18, 1920. When he was nine years old, his mother died of kidney failure. Three years later, he lost his only brother to scarlet fever. Then a few months before his twenty-first birthday, his father died of a heart attack. After burying his father, a sober Karol observed, "[By] twenty, I had already lost all the people I loved."[140]

Yet this suffering galvanized the boy, helping him find community and joy outside of his family. From a young age he gravitated toward people of different races and religions. He loved to play soccer, and since his community was populated mostly by Jews and Catholics, the games usually split along religious lines. Karol had no problem mingling with his Jewish schoolmates, even playing goalie for their team (that's where he earned his nickname, "Lolek," Polish for "the Goalkeeper"). Even as a boy, he exhibited the solidarity that would later form his legacy.

In 1938, Karol moved to Kraków, Poland, where he began studying at Jagiellonian University. At college, he became very involved in the artistic community, building strong friendships with artists, singers, and actors, and performing in clandestine theater performances.

BUILDING A CULTURE OF SOLIDARITY

"The culture of selfishness and individualism that often prevails in our society is not what builds up and leads to a more habitable world: it is the culture of solidarity that does so, seeing others not as rivals or statistics, but as brothers and sisters."[141]

— Pope Francis

But Nazi forces uprooted Karol's tranquility in 1939 when they invaded Poland. They forced able-bodied Poles to enroll in state labor, the only alternative being deportation. Karol didn't want to leave his people, so he worked various jobs. He served as a messenger, then as a miner in a limestone quarry, and finally worked in a chemical factory. The difficult and often unjust labor inspired him to become a lifelong champion of workers' rights. It also prompted his lifelong solidarity with Polish workers.

The hard labor did not suppress Karol's deeper, spiritual longings. In 1942, he visited Kraków's archbishop to express his interest in the priesthood. Karol undoubtedly knew the risks. If the Germans discovered him studying to become a priest, he would face a firing squad or perhaps deportation to Auschwitz. But that didn't deter him. He knocked on the archbishop's door, explained his desire to become a priest, and soon began classes in the archbishop's underground seminary.

Finally, after years of secret training, the archbishop of Kraków ordained Karol a priest on November 1, 1946. That set up a meteoric rise over the next few decades. Karol was made bishop in 1958, then served a key role in the Second Vatican Council (1962–1965). In 1964, Pope Paul VI named him a cardinal, and then in 1978, after the thirty-three-day papacy of John Paul I, the conclave of cardinals elected 58-year-old Karol Wojtyla as pope. He chose the name John Paul II as a nod to his predecessor. And then he embarked on a whirlwind pontificate that would shape the Church and change the world.

NINE DAYS THAT CHANGED THE WORLD

One of Pope John Paul's first decisions was to provide support and solidarity to his Polish kinsmen. Nazi forces had left Poland in 1945, and the country experienced a brief period of peace and sovereignty. But the political vacuum was soon filled by the Soviet Union. At first the communist leaders got along well with Karol Wojtyla, then a bishop in Kraków. They considered him an intelligent, personable, open-minded cleric who would compromise where needed.

But that perception soon changed when the state demanded possession of the diocesan seminary building. Other bishops may have responded with a frustrated letter, but the upstart Wojtyla marched down the street to the Communist Party headquarters and asked to speak directly with Kraków's main Communist leader.

His confidence paid off. After the meeting, he only had to relinquish one floor of space but could keep the rest of the building. From then on, the Communists knew this was a bishop who would not easily back down.

They experienced that tenacity again years later when Wojtyla was elected pope. Just months after his election, he visited his homeland for a nine-day pilgrimage in June 1979. Communist leaders hoped the visit would be fairly benign.

But they underestimated the Pope's spiritual power. He swept through Poland with remarkable fanfare, inspiring new vigor everywhere he went. During his nine-day visit, the Pope galvanized the country as over one-third of Poland witnessed him praying, speaking, and chastising the Soviet regime for repressing the country's faith. At the trip's pinnacle, John Paul stood in front of one million people in Warsaw's Victory Square, with Soviet leaders watching anxiously nearby. He proclaimed that without Christ, Poland's history is impossible to understand. Jesus Christ is crucial to its culture and vital to its flourishing, the Pope said. Therefore, in response to oppression, he roared, the people should, "Be not afraid!" Millions shouted in response, "We want God! We want God! We want God!" The people repeated this refrain for fourteen uninterrupted minutes. With dramatic flair, John Paul turned to the Soviet leaders and then gestured to the crowd, as if to say, "Listen to the people! You cannot curb their faith."

Although the Communists retained their power for another decade, those nine days served as the beginning of their end. The Pope's visit struck a mortal blow to the Polish government, the Soviet empire, and ultimately to Communism itself. And it inspired one of the most influential political movements of the twentieth-century, a movement known as "Solidarity."

THE ADVENT OF 'SOLIDARITY'

When the Pope visited Poland in 1979, his homeland was approaching a financial meltdown. The Communist-inspired "shortage economy" put stress on everyday people who were unable to purchase daily needs like bread and toilet paper. Food banks and social services dried up, and in July 1980, the Polish government raised the price of goods without raising wages. This proved to be the last straw for much of the labor force and strikes broke out across the country.

One of those strikes took place at the Lenin Shipyards in Gdansk. Led by an outspoken electrician, Lech Walesa, the workers demanded the right to form independent workers unions — which were prohibited under communism — along with freedom of the press, the official right to strike, and improvements to the state health system. The group promoted their demands through a newspaper and soon attracted tens of thousands of followers throughout Poland.

Within a few weeks, several other Polish factories shut down and joined the Gdansk workers. The situation drew international support and media coverage, and eventually the Soviet government capitulated. They signed a resolution known as the Gdansk Agreement. The resolution allowed workers to form unions, strike, and receive representation for their concerns, all of which introduced democratic features into the communist political structure.

The Gdansk victory led to a national labor union, which formed on September 17, 1980, and called itself Solidarity. The turn of events shocked the world. Nobody thought an independent trade union could exist in the Soviet Bloc. Yet within its first year of existence, over 10 million Polish people joined Solidarity or one of its suborganizations. A quarter of the country's population became members, including 80% of Poland's workforce.[142]

Over the next decade, Solidarity grew from a small union to a full-on revolutionary movement. The group never resorted to violence, but through strikes and protests, they opposed the Soviet Regime.

SOLIDARITY AT AUSCHWITZ

Fr. Maximilian Kolbe was a Polish Franciscan priest whom the Nazis captured and sent to the Auschwitz deathcamp. Two months after arriving, a man from his bunker escaped. The Nazis had a staunch rule at Auschwitz that if a man escaped, they would kill ten prisoners in retaliation. So upon learning about the escape, the Nazi commandant screamed, "You will all pay for this! Ten of you will be locked in the starvation bunker without food or water until you die."[143]

The troops selected ten men at random, including Franciszek Gajowniczek, a married man with young children. "My poor wife!" he sobbed. "My poor children! What will they do?" Hearing the man's cry, Fr. Kolbe silently stepped forward, took off his cap, and stood before the commander. He said: "I am a Catholic priest. Let me take his place. I am old. He has a wife and children."[144]

The commander agreed, and sent Kolbe and the other nine prisoners to the starvation bunker. Over the next two weeks, Kolbe cheerfully encouraged his cohorts during their tortuous decline. He prayed and sang hymns with them, and provided spiritual support as they died one by one around him. Soon, Kolbe was the only one left. On August 14, 1941, authorities decided he had lasted long enough, and they injected him with carbolic acid. Kolbe was canonized by John Paul II on October 10, 1982.

St. Maximilian Kolbe's remarkable act of solidarity — of standing with the Jewish prisoners and even giving his life for them — reminds us that solidarity is difficult and costly. And it sometimes demands everything.

A deep spirituality fueled the Solidarity movement. Workers hung pictures of the Pope throughout the Gdansk shipyard, and the strikers often prayed and sang hymns together during non-violent protests. Twelve-hundred miles away, in the Vatican, the Polish Pope closely followed the Solidarity movement's success. He regularly sent financial aid and spiritual materials back to Poland. In December 1980, the Pope invited Walensa and other Solidarity delegates to meet with him in Rome.

A month after this meeting, however, informants alerted John Paul that the Soviet Union planned to violently crush the Solidarity trade union. The Pope responded just as he did as archbishop of Kraków. He stood up boldly to the aggressors, writing a strong letter to Soviet Leader Leonid Brezhnev, urging him not to invade. The letter seemed to work. Months passed and no invasion occurred. "We were told," Walensa later revealed, "the Pope had

SOLIDARITY AND SUBSIDIARITY

The Catholic social principle of subsidiarity is a necessary counterpart to solidarity. Subsidiarity holds that a matter ought to be handled by the smallest, lowest, or least centralized authority capable. For example, the federal government shouldn't meddle with problems states can solve, states shouldn't be solving problems that cities can solve, and so on.

The two principles flow together, as Pope Benedict XVI explained in his encyclical Caritas in Veritate:

"The principle of subsidiarity must remain closely linked to the principle of solidarity and vice versa, since the former without the latter gives way to social privatism, while the latter without the former gives way to paternalist social assistance that is demeaning to those in need."[148]

Solidarity ensures all people are taken care of while subsidiarity prevents people from becoming faceless objects of charity. When both principles flourish together, they result in a more balanced, effective, and personal bond of charity.

warned the Soviets that if they entered Poland he would fly to Poland and stay with the Polish people."[145]

The next year, in 1981, Pope John Paul devoted his second encyclical to work, titling it *Laborem Exercens* ("On Human Labor"). He sprinkled it with many references to solidarity. It was undoubtedly a hint of encouragement to the Polish people in their struggle for freedom.

The encyclical also affirmed that solidarity offered a far better framework for human society than Marxist communism. The latter posited "class struggle" as the motor of social change, pitting people against each other in order to promote progress. But solidarity encouraged people to work *together* toward progress, seeing injustice as the common enemy.

By late 1981, the communists decided to crack down on Solidarity. On December 13, the Soviet military declared martial law and arrested the leaders of the movement. This time, Pope John Paul responded not with personal confrontation, or with an angry letter, but with a global call to prayer. He hosted a vigil service at the Vatican, which ended with a plea to end the persecution.

Once again, John Paul's efforts proved successful. The Soviets released Walesa and the other Solidarity leaders from prison, Solidarity was reinstated, and over the next eight years, the Communist bloc unraveled, quicker than anyone expected and, shockingly, without a single bullet fired.

After Pope John Paul's visits to Poland in 1983 and 1987, the final strands of Soviet communism came undone in 1989. That proved to be a banner year for the Pope. Within just a few months, the Berlin Wall collapsed, Poland experienced its first free election, and the new Soviet president Mikhail Gorbachev visited the Pope.

During their meeting, Gorbachev committed to new political and social reforms. He also applauded John Paul's role in the Cold War, describing the Pope as "a providential man."[146] He even claimed, "The collapse of the Iron Curtain would have been impossible without John Paul II."[147]

Opinions still vary on how much Pope John Paul affected the downfall of Communism, but most agree he was an indispensable figure. His ability to peacefully defeat the Soviet statesmen, and inspire Poland to join together in faith, is a testament to the power of solidarity.

SOLIDARITY WITH OTHER GROUPS

Throughout the rest of his pontificate, Pope John Paul also encouraged unity with many other groups. He was especially committed to solidarity among Christians, reaching out to Orthodox, Anglican, and Lutheran leaders. In 1995, he wrote the encyclical *Ut Unum Sint* ("That They May be One") in which he affirmed the Catholic Church's desire to unite with other Christians. In one remarkable passage he even asked non-Catholic Christians to help him redesign the papacy to serve as an office of unity for the whole Church of Christ.

The Pope also reached out to other world religions. In 1985, John Paul addressed 80,000 Muslim youths on the importance of peace between Christianity and Islam. He also made several moves to strengthen solidarity with Judaism, including becoming the first pope to visit Rome's synagogue and finalizing a landmark agreement between Israel and the Holy See, which led to full diplomatic relations. In March 2000, he visited the Holy Land, and while at the Western Wall he inserted a prayer between the stones that invoked "a new era of fraternal dialogue in the third millennium."

John Paul's remarkable life and pontificate, marked by solidarity from start to finish, came to a slow end on April 2, 2005. After twenty-five years as pope, two assassination attempts, several cancer scares, and a four-year struggle with Parkinson's disease, John Paul died quietly in the papal apartments. Shortly before his death, he learned that tens of thousands of people were holding a vigil for him in St. Peter's square. In response, the Pope who had traveled around the world delivered one final message for the pilgrims: "I have searched for you, and now you have come to me, and I thank you."[149]

LESSONS FROM ST. JOHN PAUL II

Neither you nor I will probably ever share the global influence of John Paul II. But we can still draw three helpful lessons from his life regarding solidarity. First, John Paul demonstrates that solidarity is difficult. We sometimes have romantic visions in which warring countries or feuding family members reunite easily and quickly. But building solidarity is hard work. The U.S. Bishops affirmed this in their 1997 document, *Called to Global Solidarity*:

> "Solidarity ... drives the comfortable and secure to take risks for the victims of tyranny and war. It calls those who are strong to care for those who are weak and vulnerable across the spectrum of human life. It opens homes and hearts to those in flight from terror and to migrants whose daily toil supports affluent lifestyles."[150]

Pope John Paul II knew that solidarity requires sacrifice. He often pursued it at great risk. He supported the Polish workers, and stood with unpopular groups, even though his actions provoked serious threats to his life. Solidarity is rarely cheap, but as John Paul showed, it's always worth the cost.

A second lesson from John Paul's life is that solidarity is not just local — it stretches across the globe. In his encyclical *Centesimus Annus*, the Pope referenced the Bible's call to worldwide solidarity:

> "Sacred Scripture continually speaks to us of an active commitment to our neighbor and demands of us a shared responsibility for all of humanity. This duty is not limited to one's own family, nation, or state, but extends progressively to all ... so no one can consider himself extraneous or indifferent to the lot of another member of the human family."[151]

The central question of solidarity is the question Cain asked in Genesis: "Am I my brother's keeper?" (Gn 4:9). To ask it another way: "Are we responsible for the fate of the world's poor? Do we have duties to suffering people in far-off places? Must we respond to the needs of suffering refugees in distant nations? Are we keepers of the creation for future generations?"[152]

For John Paul II and for all followers of Jesus, the answer is a resounding yes. The Lord's command to "love others as I have loved you" links us to people across the globe, from New York to Rwanda, Germany to Bosnia, and China to Vietnam.

One practical way that some parishes live out this global solidarity is through a process known as "twinning." A parish in the United States develops an ongoing relationship with a parish in another part of the world, creating a bridge of faith and mutual support. Over 1,700 parishes in the United States currently participate in "twinning," and if your parish has not yet participated, you might consider suggesting the idea to your pastor.

Finally, Pope John Paul shows us the difference between solidarity and compassion. Sometimes, especially in the digital age, it's easy to confuse these two expressions of charity. Compassion literally means "to suffer with" and serves as a powerful sign of unity. But solidarity, while it includes compassion, is much more than that. It's not just a spontaneous movement of the heart but also a decision to take action and join together with another person or group. As Pope John Paul noted:

> "[Solidarity] is not a feeling of vague compassion or shallow distress at the misfortunes of so many people, both near and far. On the contrary, it is a firm and persevering determination to commit oneself to the common good; that is to say, to the good of all and of each individual, because we are all really responsible for all."[153]

The next time we encounter a struggling friend or family member, we can certainly express support and compassion, but then ask ourselves, what can I do to help alleviate this situation? It may be some small action, or it may be to simply pray for them, but what concrete action can I take to express my solidarity? Asking these types of questions moves us past "vague compassion" and into the "firm and persevering" commitment that Pope John Paul encouraged and demonstrated throughout his life.

CHAPTER 12
ST. DAMIEN
OF MOLOKAI

I remember the first time I discovered St. Damien of Molokai. I saw a picture of him taken shortly before his death. By that time, leprosy had already eaten away much of his flesh. His puffy forehead sagged over his eyes and his cheeks appeared to be melting off his face. Yet what most captivated me was his one open eye, which peered out from the disfigurement with a remarkable serenity. This wasn't a man who was angered or saddened by his disease. He appeared poised and resolute. As I came to know St. Damien's life story, I quickly discovered where that confidence came from.

Jozef de Veuster was born in Belgium on January 3, 1840, the last of seven children. As a boy, Jozef yearned to be a great missionary like St. Peter or St. Paul. He wanted to travel the world and preach the Gospel to people who had never heard about Jesus. He decided his best path toward this goal would be joining a religious order. So as a teenager he followed his older brother Auguste into the Congregation of the Sacred Hearts of Jesus and Mary. In 1860, he took his first vows, choosing the religious name Brother Damien.

Initially, Damien's superiors didn't think he would make a very good priest, since he lacked formal education. But as he progressed in his studies he changed their perception. For example, Damien displayed a mastery of Latin, which he picked up from his brother. And he also impressed his superiors by praying every day before a picture of St. Francis Xavier, the patron of missionaries. Damien never wavered in his commitment to evangelize the world. All he needed was a chance, someone to send him out on a mission.

That day came in early 1864, though unexpectedly. Damien's brother, Auguste, was supposed to sail out for Honolulu, Hawaii, where the Congregation was establishing a mission. But Auguste became ill and could not make the trip. The superiors asked whether Damien would like to go instead. I imagine it must have been a thrilling moment for Damien, which probably caused him to leap for joy before darting onto the ship.

After a long time at sea the ship landed at Honolulu Harbor on March 19, 1864. Damien hardly had a chance to settle in before, two days later, he was ordained a priest in the island's cathedral. Then after a few months of surveying the land, the superiors assigned Damien to their mission at North Kohala, the upper tip of Hawaii's largest island.

"YOU COME AND SEE MY ROOM"

Millions of people admire Mother Teresa of Calcutta not only for her remarkable service toward the poor, but also for the way she entered into solidarity with them. This anecdote from a 1989 interview with *Time* magazine illustrates this capacity:

Time **magazine:** There's been some criticism of the very severe regimen under which you and your Sisters live.

Mother Teresa: We chose that. That is the difference between us and the poor. Because what will bring us closer to our poor people? How can we be truthful to them if we lead a different life? If we have everything possible that money can give, that the world can give, then what is our connection to the poor? What language will I speak to them? Now if the people tell me it is so hot, I can say you come and see my room.

Time **magazine:** Just as hot?

Mother Teresa: Much hotter even, because there is a kitchen underneath. A man came and stayed here as a cook at the children's home. He was rich before and became very poor. Lost everything. He came and said, "Mother Teresa, I cannot eat that food." I said, "I am eating it every day." He looked at me and said, "You eat it too? All right, I will eat it also." And he left perfectly happy. Now if I could not tell him the truth, that man would have remained bitter. He would never have accepted his poverty. He would never have accepted to have that food when he was used to other kinds of food. That helped him to forgive, to forget.[154]

"I MAKE MYSELF A LEPER"

When Damien arrived in Hawaii in 1864, he found an island-community beset by infections. Over the years, travelers and seamen had introduced diseases such as influenza and syphilis. Yet none were as bad as Hansen's Disease, more commonly known as leprosy. First reported in Hawaii in 1840, leprosy devastated people in many ways. First, because the disease was highly contagious and untreatable until the 1930s, people contracting it had no hope of recovery. This often led to deep depression among its sufferers. Second, leprosy caused a progressive degeneration of their skin, eyes, and limbs. It thus disfigured people and eventually immobilized them. Finally, few diseases isolated people from their communities as much as leprosy. Sufferers were seen as outcasts and cautioned to stay away from everyone else.

In 1866, to curb the spread of the disease, Hawaiian authorities decided to consign lepers to an isolated community on the island of Molokai. On three sides, the colony, called Kalaupapa, bordered the Pacific Ocean, and the fourth side featured massive, 1,600-foot cliffs. Once the lepers were out of sight and no longer a threat to the general population, the government turned a blind eye to their basic needs. Shipments of food and supplies slowed down, and the government removed most of its personnel. The result was a highly dysfunctional community marked by poverty, alcoholism, violence, and promiscuity.

Puritan missionaries became convinced that leprosy stemmed from the people's licentiousness. But Damien knew that wasn't true. He believed the people on Molokai were basically good, not corrupt, and that sin did not cause the spread of the disease.

In time, Damien came to see the neglected colony as the answer to his boyhood longings. He asked the local bishop for permission to go to Molokai, and the bishop not only granted approval, but personally accompanied Damien to the island. He introduced Damien to the 816 community members as "one who will be a father to you and who loves you so much that he does not hesitate to become one of you, to live and die with you."[155]

This introduction didn't surprise Damien, who had no illusions about what his mission would entail. He knew working in the disease-ridden colony virtually guaranteed that he would become infected, too. Yet he never wavered in his commitment.

THE 501ST LEPER

Ven. Fulton Sheen was one of the twentieth century's most effective evangelists. Through radio and television he brought the Gospel to tens of millions of people.

But in addition to his media work, he also served as the national director of the Society for the Propagation of the Faith. This position took him on numerous missions to distant people around the world. And one of those trips, an experience of solidarity in Africa, had a lasting effect:

"On one of my visits to the missions, I went to a leper colony in Buluba, Africa, where there were 500 lepers. I brought with me 500 silver crucifixes, intending to give one to each of the lepers — this symbol of the Lord's Redemption. The first one who came to meet me had his left arm eaten off at the elbow by the disease. He put out his right hand and it was the most foul, noisome mass of corruption I ever saw. I held the silver crucifix above it, and dropped it. It was swallowed up in that volcano of leprosy.

"All of a sudden there were 501 lepers in that camp; I was the 501st because I had taken that symbol of God's identification with man and refused to identify myself with someone who was a thousand times better on the inside than I. Then it came over me the awful thing I had done. I dug my fingers into his leprosy, took out the crucifix and pressed it into his hand. And so on, for all the other 499 lepers. From that moment on I learned to love them."[156]

THE MOLOKAI LEPER COLONY

At first, the conditions around the lepers proved overwhelming. Damien often felt as if he had opened a door to hell. Victims wandered about, their bodies in ruin and their constant coughing the island's most familiar sound. Damien could hardly bear the stench:

"Many a time in fulfilling my priestly duties at the lepers' homes, I have been obliged, not only to close my nostrils, but to remain outside to breathe fresh air. To counteract the bad smell, I got myself accustomed to the use of tobacco. The smell of the pipe preserved me somewhat from carrying in my clothes the obnoxious odor of our lepers."[157]

Eventually Damien overcame the distressing sights and smells. His superiors had given him strict advice: "Do not touch them. Do not allow them to touch you. Do not eat with them." But Damien made the decision to transcend his fear of contagion and enter into solidarity with the Molokai lepers. He committed to visit every leper on the island and to inquire of their needs.

One early realization was that to show the lepers the value of their lives, he had to first demonstrate the value of their deaths. So he built a fence around the local cemetery, which pigs and dogs regularly scavenged. He also constructed coffins and dug graves, committing that each leper, even if marginalized throughout his life, would receive a decent burial upon death. This had a remarkably uplifting effect on the community.

Damien also devoted his attention to the sick. He brought the sacraments to bedridden lepers. He washed their bodies and bandaged their wounds. He tidied their rooms and did all he could to make them as comfortable as possible.

What surprised the lepers most was that Damien *touched* them. Other missionaries and doctors shrank from the lepers. In fact, one local doctor only changed bandages with his cane. But Damien not only touched the lepers, he also embraced them, he dined with them, he put his thumb on their forehead to anoint them, and he placed the Eucharist on their tongues. All of these actions spoke volumes to the dejected lepers. They showed that Damien didn't want to serve them from afar; he wanted to become one of them.

Damien was careful never to present himself as a messianic figure, soaring in from a higher, more privileged position. He invited lepers to join in the work, turning his service to the community into an act of solidarity. He had them help build everything from coffins to cottages. When the colony expanded along the island's peninsula, his leper friends helped construct a new road. Under his supervision, the lepers even blasted away rocks on the shoreline to create a new docking facility. Damien also taught the lepers to farm, raise animals, play musical instruments, and sing. Although the lepers were used to being patronized or bullied, Damien spread among them a new cheer and sense of worth.

This refreshing spirit impressed visitors to the island. "I had gone to Molokai expecting to find it scarcely less dreadful than hell itself," wrote Englishman Edward Clifford in 1888, "and the cheerful people, the lovely landscapes, and comparatively painless life were all surprises. These poor people seemed singularly happy."[158]

Despite the idyllic community Damien had built through a decade of work, the moment he feared finally arrived in December 1884. One day, while soaking his feet in extremely hot water, Damien experienced no sensation of heat or pain — a tell-tale sign that he had contracted leprosy. The disease quickly developed, causing Damien to write to his bishop with the news: "Its marks are seen on my left cheek and ear, and my eyebrows are beginning to fall. I shall soon be completely disfigured. I have no doubt whatever of the nature of my illness, but I am calm and resigned and very happy in the midst of my people. The good God knows what is best for my sanctification. I daily repeat from my heart, 'Thy will be done.'"[159]

Soon, he also wrote home to his brother: "I make myself a leper with the lepers to gain all to Jesus Christ."[160]

Even before contracting the disease, Damien spoke of himself and the people of Molokai as "we lepers." He identified closely with those he came to serve and thus, before and after the disease, offered a powerful, concrete expression of solidarity.

THE COWBOY PRIEST

While Damien served the lepers in Hawaii, another Catholic saint carried out similar work a continent away. Bl. José Gabriel Brochero (1840–1914) was known throughout Argentina for the assistance he gave to the sick and dying during a cholera epidemic in 1867.

Yet today he's best remembered for his service to Argentinian lepers. Like Damien, José built churches, chapels, and schools with the help of leprous peasants. He traveled from village to village on a mule, visiting their homes and meeting their personal needs, all of which earned him the nickname, "Cowboy Priest."

When Pope Francis beatified Bl. José on September 14, 2013, over 150,000 people attended the ceremony, including thousands dressed in the cowboy poncho the saint wore when serving his leper friends. The Pope used the occasion to praise Jose's solidarity and missionary drive:

"[Fr. Brochero] did not stay in the parish office, but instead pressed on, ranging through the parish atop his mule, becoming ill with leprosy, seeking his flock, bringing faith to the street. This is what Jesus wants today: missionary disciples who take faith out onto the streets!...

"Let us allow Brochero to enter today, mule and all, into the homes of our hearts, inviting us to prayer, to the encounter with Jesus; let him deliver us from our bondage so that we too might go out to seek our brother, to touch the flesh of Christ in those who suffer and who need God's love."

A CALL TO SOLIDARITY

"Today's celebration is also a call to solidarity. While Damien was among the sick, he could say in his heart: 'Our Lord will give me the graces I need to carry my cross and follow him, even to our special Calvary at Kalawao.' The certainty that the only things that count are love and the gift of self was his inspiration and the source of his happiness. The apostle of the lepers is a shining example of how the love of God does not take us away from the world. Far from it: the love of Christ makes us love our brothers and sisters even to the point of giving up our lives for them."

— Pope John Paul II, homily at the beatification of St. Damien of Molokai

PATRON OF LEPERS

In the final act of oneness with his poor flock, Damien died on April 15, 1889. The colonists buried him beneath the small tree that had provided his only shelter when he first arrived.

Shortly after his death, Charles Hyde, a Presbyterian minister in Honolulu, wrote a scathing article attacking Damien's image. He dismissed Damien as "a course, dirty man, headstrong and bigoted," and accused of him of violating his vow of chastity.[161]

The accusations were, of course, false. And Damien found a surprising defender in Robert Louis Stevenson, the acclaimed author of classics like *Treasure Island*. Stevenson was living in Samoa when he read Hyde's letter and he decided to visit the Molokai leper colony to ask questions about the priest's ministry. Based on what he learned, he published a very long letter reprimanding Hyde, affirming that while Damien may have been rough around the edges, he was also "superb with generosity, residual candour, and fundamental good humour.... A man with all the grime and paltriness of mankind, but a saint and hero all the more for that."[162] In the letter, he also predicted that within a hundred years Damien would be proclaimed a saint.

Stevenson may have been slightly off regarding the time frame but was otherwise correct. On October 11, 2009, Pope Benedict XVI canonized Damien in the presence of several kings, queens, and dignitaries, including Belgian King Albert II. From that moment on, he would become known not by his homeland, but by the island community he served — St. Damien of Molokai, patron of lepers.

LESSONS FROM ST. DAMIEN OF MOLOKAI

We can learn several lessons from Damien's magnificent example. First, he affirms that solidarity is two-pronged: it shares in suffering, but it also helps alleviate it. Damien saw nothing glamorous in leprosy. In fact, he hated the disease. While he understood the spiritual benefit of suffering, he never considered leprosy something valuable in itself.

Therefore, while sharing the burden of the disease's dreadful effects, he did everything he could to ease the sufferers' pain.

One practical way to follow Damien's lead in this way is through Catholic Relief Service's annual Rice Bowl program. Each Friday during Lent, the charity invites Catholics to set aside the money they would have spent on dinner, and instead cook a simple, low-priced meal from a third-world country. Catholic Relief Services provides the recipes and collection boxes, and at the end of Lent they gather and send the funds to hungry communities around the world. This simple practice is one way to unite in true solidarity, sharing simple meals with people in need while providing support to help alleviate their hunger.

A second lesson from Damien is that solidarity requires an active choice. It's easy to think we'll fall passively into solidarity. After all, many of our friendships or relationships with coworkers began without much effort. But the sort of solidarity that Catholic social teaching advocates is an active pursuit. It requires taking regular, intentional steps into communion with others, even when they lead us into uncomfortable situations.

Damien surely commiserated with the Molokai lepers before he landed in Hawaii. But it wasn't until he touched them, ate with them, worked with them — and ultimately died with them — that he entered into solidarity. By his life and death he showed that solidarity is an action, not a feeling, and it requires more than mere sentiment.

Third, like many saints before him, Damien witnesses to the spiritual power that comes from rooting solidarity in the Eucharist. Writing to a friend, Damien confessed:

"I find my consolation in the one and only companion who will never leave me, that is, our Divine Saviour in the Holy Eucharist.... It is at the foot of the altar that we find the strength necessary in this isolation of ours. Without the Blessed Sacrament a position like mine would be unbearable. But, having Our Lord at my side, I continue always to be happy and content."[163]

For Damien, solidarity is both a physical and a spiritual pursuit. The more he cultivated solidarity with God, the greater his capacity for sharing it with his brother and sister lepers. This lesson reveals that the deepest kind of solidarity is grounded in divine love.

One final lesson is how Damien showed solidarity with his leper friends by treating them with honor — for example, he gave them self-respect by involving them in the work of building roads, cottages, and public buildings. We should show the same kind of solidarity with our marginalized friends, involving them in service with us. By inviting our brothers and sisters to participate instead of just receiving a handout, we ensure that solidarity does not devolve into patronizing.

CARE FOR CREATION

We show our respect for the Creator by our stewardship of creation. Care for the earth is not just an Earth Day slogan; it is a requirement of our faith. We are called to protect people and the planet, living our faith in relationship with all of God's creation. **This environmental challenge has fundamental moral and ethical dimensions that cannot be ignored.**[164]

CHAPTER 13
ST. GILES

You might be surprised that this last section on care for creation doesn't feature St. Francis of Assisi or St. Kateri Tekakwitha, the two saints we most often associate with the environment. With Francis' animal friends and Kateri's Native American heritage, they seem like excellent examples. But while both inspire in countless ways, I wasn't sure they offered the best model for this theme.

I instead chose two other saints who expressed a remarkable sense that creation is a great gift from God, a gift that we're meant to protect, cultivate, and share. Both saints, St. Giles and St. Isidore the Laborer, embody Catholic teaching on creation.

ANIMALS AND RICHES

St. Giles is one of the more popular saints in Europe, but his life is shrouded in mystery and legend. Perhaps the only fact we know for certain is that he was born in Athens, Greece, likely in the mid-seventh century. Giles was a dreamy, quiet boy who loved to wander the countryside. With no companions but the animals, birds, and flowers, he'd spend hours enjoying God's creation. The woodland creatures gradually befriended Giles, and even the wildest animals would come within arm's reach. Some accounts note that animals seemed to listen when he talked to them, as if they could understand what he said.[165] If nothing else, the animals certainly understood that Giles loved them and would protect them and their surrounding land.

They knew this because Giles often healed the wounds of his animal friends. On any given day he could be found mending a bird's broken wing or binding a rabbit's foot that had been torn in a trap. The animals seemed to trust Giles and would lie still while he cured them, even though it hurt.

Unfortunately, Giles' idyllic childhood ended when he lost both of his parents at a young age. They were enormously wealthy, and they left Giles a large inheritance: castles, vineyards, horses, gold, and silver. But Giles didn't need any of the luxuries. Among his friends, animals, and small plot of land, he had everything he could want. He decided to give the inheritance to God, donating the property to local abbeys and hospitals and sending the money to poor families.

Giles' remarkable charity scandalized many of his friends. They pleaded with him to keep the wealth and live luxuriously. With his position, they noted, he could marry the daughter of a baron, a count, or a king who could then provide him an heir to whom he could leave his possessions and carry on his name. But if Giles was just going to give it all away, they joked, he might as well become a monk!

Surprisingly, Giles agreed. After giving away the last of his property, he set out on the road, aiming to become a hermit in the woods. His friends were shocked and convicted, as Giles' decision exposed their own warped view of creation. His friends gauged a person's success by how much land he owned or how many animals were under his control. But Giles had a more sociable relationship with creation. He shunned the unnecessary domination of animals, refusing to wear their skins as clothes or even using them for transportation. He saw the land as a gift from God meant to be shared and cultivated rather than property to be owned, exploited, and left as an inheritance. These radical views, which were very uncommon in his day, provoked new reflection on how Christians should relate to the environment.

HOW SHOULD WE TREAT THE ENVIRONMENT?

We fulfill God's commission with regard to creation when we care for the earth, with its biological laws, its variety of species, its natural beauty, and its dwindling resources, as a living space and preserve it, so that future generations also can live well on earth.

In the book of Genesis, God says, "Be fruitful and multiply, and fill the earth and subdue it; and have dominion over the fish of the sea and over the birds of the air and over every living thing that moves upon the earth" (Gen 1:28). Having "dominion over the earth" does not mean having an absolute right to dispose arbitrarily of animate and inanimate nature, animals, and plants.

NATURE'S FRIEND

Giles eventually made it to the coast and sailed westward until he reached Marseilles, France. There he found a lonely cave, away from crowds. A clear stream flowed nearby. Giles awoke each morning to the chirping of birds, and soon animals from the woods ventured close to share his meals. But of all his many companions, the one Giles loved most was a gentle white doe. After its first encounter with Giles, the doe rarely left him. It lay close to him when he slept and walked side-by-side wherever he went. Giles helped gather food for the doe while it nourished him with its milk.

Besides the milk, Giles chose only to eat whatever fruits and vegetation he could find. He lived as a vegetarian for many years. Catholic ecologist William L. Patenaude observes that "this in itself [was] a sort of critique of the prevalent banquet and hunting culture of his age."[167]

It seemed like nothing could disturb Giles' peaceful, prayerful life, which he lived in communion with the animals and the earth. But then one day a loud noise shocked Giles out of his morning prayer. Listening closer, he heard men's shouting, the sounds of galloping horses, and the blasts of a hunter's horn. Giles looked around for the doe. He didn't see her in the cave and so he ran outside, only to see the hunting party racing upon her.

The doe leapt up and dashed through the field toward him, disappearing into the cave just as one of the huntsmen sent an arrow flying after her. The huntsmen arrived at the cave opening, dismounted, and went to see what had become of the doe. But when they walked in they found Giles kneeling in front of her, sheltering the terrified animal that had fled to him for refuge. Then the hunters noticed Giles' hand, which was raised to shield the poor doe. An arrow had pierced it.

The huntsmen hung their heads in shame. One of the men stepped forward and Giles was surprised to see it was the King of the Franks, who ruled the land we now call France. The King asked who Giles was, and the hermit explained that he was just a simple man, interested only in praying to God and serving his creation. This impressed the King. He tried to persuade Giles to leave his cave and return to the palace where he could serve as the King's spiritual director. Yet Giles kindly refused, saying he wanted to be left alone in his woodland cave. The King offered a compromise: if Giles would agree to disciple other young men in the way of holiness, he would build Giles a monastery in the woods, which he would furnish with anything Giles required. Aware of how much good this might do, the hermit reluctantly agreed and began planning a small community centered on the Rule of St. Benedict.

MONKS OF MEDIEVAL EUROPE

St. Giles wasn't the only medieval monk who cared for creation. Monasteries across Europe helped save agriculture when nobody else would. With their special emphasis on manual labor, the Benedictine monks were particularly influential. Their work led Francois Guizot, a nineteenth-century French historian who was fairly anti-Catholic, to write, "The Benedictine monks were the agriculturists of Europe; they cleared it on a large scale, associating agriculture with preaching."[168] Another historian observed, "Wherever they came, they converted the wilderness into a cultivated country; they pursued the breeding of cattle and agriculture, labored with their own hands, drained morasses, and cleared away forests."[169]

The monks were particularly effective in reclaiming swampland. The prevailing view of most people was that swamps were sources of pestilence and utterly worthless. But the monks thrived in these locations, moving in and converting the discarded land into fertile beds of agriculture.

In his book *How the Catholic Church Built Western Civilization*, historian Thomas Woods notes, "Wherever they went, the monks introduced crops, industries, or production methods with which the people had not been previously familiar. Here they would introduce the rearing of cattle and horses, there the brewing of beer or the raising of bees or fruit."[170]

Although we still remember the medieval monks for their scholastic achievements, we must not forget their remarkable contribution toward renewing a Catholic ecology.

THE POPE'S BLESSING

Giles oversaw the building of the monastery promised by the King, and as soon as it was finished it began attracting a community. It also drew the attention of other rulers, including Charles Martel, who ruled Frankland at the turn of the eighth century. Martel summoned Giles to his palace for spiritual advice on a serious matter and the hermit agreed. He made the long and difficult journey to Orleans, and once there, before even talking with Martel to determine his problem, he explained that he would only find relief after confessing a particularly serious, but secret sin. The shocked ruler followed Giles' advice, found great peace, and then sent him home with many tokens of gratitude.

After returning home for a short period, Giles set out again, this time for Rome to meet the Pope and attain a blessing for his small community. The Pope granted Giles' wish and imparted his blessing, along with other special privileges. He also gave Giles two large, beautifully-carved doors made of cedar wood, which were designed to fit Giles' woodland monastery. Some legends say Giles threw the doors into the Tiber river in Rome, on which they floated downstream to the sea. When Giles returned to France, the doors lay waiting on a nearby beach, close to his monastery.

Giles died peacefully in his monastery, tucked in the fields he loved so much. In the following centuries he would become one of Europe's most beloved saints. People relished the thought of this peaceful old saint who lived in the woods, and protected sad and suffering creatures. Giles was the only non-martyr included among the Fourteen Holy Helpers, a group of saints honored by towns in the Rhineland. Also, thanks in part to the Crusaders, his story spread far to other countries. This brought many pilgrims to his monastery shrine where they prayed, sought healing, and asked for Giles' intercession. The monastery remains a popular stopping point on pilgrimage routes to Compostela and the Holy Land.

Today, at least fifteen French cities and provinces take their name from Giles, along with twenty-four hospitals and at least 160 churches in England — especially those built in fields or near green woods. Though he doesn't officially carry the title, it's no stretch to consider him the patron saint of ecology.

THE GREEN POPE

Perhaps no pope in history has written or spoken as often about creation as Pope Benedict XVI. Dubbed "The Green Pope" by some commentators, Benedict has taken several steps to promote natural stewardship. One of the more noteworthy projects during his pontificate involved planting a 37-acre forest in Hungary and installing a solar cooling system in the Vatican's main cafeteria. The projects reduced and offset the Vatican's carbon emissions, transforming Vatican City into the world's first carbon-neutral state.

Yet we must not confuse the Pope for a secular environmentalist. Perhaps the most distinctive feature of his care for creation is that it places the human person at its center. A truly Catholic ecology doesn't seek to reduce the number of humans in order to protect the environment. It sees people, animals, and land as interdependent and indispensable to each other.

As Pope Benedict noted during a 2009 general audience, "The Earth is indeed a precious gift of the Creator who, in designing its intrinsic order, has given us bearings that guide us as stewards of his creation. Precisely from within this framework, the Church considers matters concerning the environment and its protection intimately linked to the theme of integral human development."[171]

Besides ensuring that humans remain at the center of our environmental concern, the Pope also encouraged people to summon up a new urgency for this stewardship. Speaking to over half a million young Catholics in 2007, he said: "Before it's too late, we need to make courageous choices that will recreate a strong alliance between man and Earth. We need a decisive 'yes' to care for creation and a strong commitment to reverse those trends that risk making a situation of decay irreversible."[172]

Saints like Giles and Isidore demonstrate a Catholic care for creation, but the Green Pope has provided a rich theology of the environment.

LESSONS FROM ST. GILES

Giles' great love for creation offers many lessons. First, he highlights the connection between our consumption and the environment around us. Giles became deeply concerned by the excessive feasting he saw throughout seventh-century France, and especially the violence it did to the natural world. He saw how this lifestyle threatened animals, exploited the land, and created ecological imbalances. Therefore, he chose at an early age to reject this hyper-consumerism and live a simpler, more balanced life. We can follow his example by using only those resources we really need — especially in regards to food, water, and electricity — and not indulging in excessive consumption.

Second, Giles demonstrates that we're responsible for protecting the land and animals around us. God provided the natural world to us as a gift, something for our own benefit. But he also calls us to steward this creation. Giles understood this well, and that's what inspired him to care for injured and hunted animals and cultivate the land so that it could produce crops well into the future. Unlike his baron friends who exploited their natural resources in order to maintain their wealth and status, Giles exhibited a more humble relationship to creation.

Third, and maybe most importantly, Giles teaches that our responsibility to the environment should be grounded on the Gospel. Giles was first and foremost a Catholic who viewed his ecology through the lens of faith. For instance, his reading of Genesis 1:28–29 prompted him to only eat vegetation and seed-bearing fruit. His understanding of the Beatitudes led him to embrace a simple home, simple food, and a simple life. This isn't to say that all Catholics have to live like St. Giles. I myself won't be giving up meat anytime soon, nor drinking milk from a white doe. But it does mean that our view of the environment should be shaped by the Gospel more than politics, money, or convenience.

CHAPTER 14

ST. ISIDORE
THE FARMER

I 've always been drawn to simple saints. I like the plain heroes who work ordinary jobs — doorkeepers, cooks, homemakers, laborers — men and women who aren't concerned with achieving great wealth, honor, or power. They're content to carry out their small responsibilities with intention and dignity, unconcerned that most of the world won't notice them.

That's why I'm drawn to St. Isidore, a poor, unassuming farmer. He was not well-educated; he couldn't match the intellectual acumen of St. Augustine or St. Ambrose. But what he lacked in smarts he made up for in devotion. Isidore relished his grueling but simple work in the fields because it gave him time to reflect and pray. He found God at the farm, feeding his soul while stewarding the land.

I am especially attracted to Isidore because he's one of our few and earliest married saints. His wife, Maria de la Cabeza, was equally pious and joined her husband in becoming canonized. Isidore's simple, earthy spirituality and his imitable marriage caused him to become one of Spain's most revered saints and a patron for those who care for creation.

BECOMING PROTECTORS OF CREATION

Since the start of his papacy, Pope Francis has exhibited a strong concern for creation. During his installation homily, which he preached on the solemnity of St.

Joseph, the Pope explained how Jesus' earthly father models for us the role of protector — not just for the Holy Family, but for all the world:

"The vocation of being a 'protector' ... means protecting all creation, the beauty of the created world, as the Book of Genesis tells us and as Saint Francis of Assisi showed us. It means respecting each of God's creatures and respecting the environment in which we live....

"Whenever human beings fail to live up to this responsibility, whenever we fail to care for creation and for our brothers and sisters, the way is opened to destruction and hearts are hardened....

"Please, I would like to ask all those who have positions of responsibility in economic, political, and social life, and all men and women of goodwill: let us be 'protectors' of creation, protectors of God's plan inscribed in nature, protectors of one another and of the environment."[173]

READING BOTH OF GOD'S BOOKS

Isidore was born in Madrid around the year 1070 to poor but devout parents. He spent his life as a servant laborer, working the fields for a wealthy landowner named Juan de Vargas. Isidore's poverty didn't discourage him from sharing the little he had with others. He regularly split his meals into smaller portions to feed his fellow workers. From a young age, he also developed a strong bond with the farm animals, never treating them violently or disrespectfully. This close relationship helped Isidore excel in the field of animal husbandry. When he first started working for de Vargas, the animal stock was fairly small. But within a short time, Isidore had greatly increased the size of the herd.

We know the details of Isidore's early life with relative confidence, but as with St. Giles, it's hard to tell where truth ends and legend begins. His biography wasn't recorded until 150 years after his death, which allowed the author to tell some of the wondrous anecdotes that had accumulated over time. For example, each morning Isidore attended Mass in Madrid before heading to the fields, often lingering in prayer afterward. His envious coworkers complained to their master, claiming Isidore's spiritual activities caused him to drag in late for work. The master decided to investigate. He approached Isidore about the issue and the simple farmer did not deny the charges: "Sir, it may be true that I am later at my work than some of the other laborers, but I do my utmost to make up for the few minutes snatched for prayer; I pray you compare my work with theirs, and if you find I have defrauded you in the least, gladly will I make amends by paying you out of my private store."[174]

The skeptical master decided to hide himself one morning so that he could observe when Isidore arrived. Sure enough, Isidore showed up late and the master emerged to chastise him. But as he did, he saw an astonishing sight in the distance. A group of snow white oxen tilled the fields in Isidore's place, driven by angelic beings. The master quickly dropped the issue.

On another occasion, the master looked out into the fields and saw what appeared to be two angels plowing the fields, this time on either side of Isidore. He thought his eyes deceived him until he measured Isidore's production that day and discovered that it equaled that of three average laborers.

Though likely legendary, these two accounts point to Isidore's synthesis of work, prayer, and the environment. For him, the spiritual life was deeply connected to creation. One could not thrive while the other was ignored. Theologians have often suggested that God wrote two books, the Bible and the Book of Nature. As Isidore knew, we're at our best when we read both.

MARTYR OF THE AMAZON

Like Isidore, Sister Dorothy Stang was raised on a farm in a traditional Catholic family. After living in Dayton, Ohio, for the first thirty-six years of her life, she moved to Brazil in 1966 to serve poor farmers. There she worked with the Pastoral Land Commission, a Catholic organization that fights for rural workers and peasants, protecting them from greedy ranchers and destructive farming practices. Dorothy expressed a special concern for the Amazon rainforests, which were under constant threat from large corporations. She liked to wear a t-shirt that read, "The end of the forest is the end of our life." Dorothy knew that exploitive deforestation not only threatened the natural order, it represented a devastating attack on God's creation.

As Dorothy became more vocal and active in her opposition, she attracted many enemies. On the morning of February 12, 2005, she awoke early and walked to a community meeting concerning the rights of the Amazon. Along the way, two armed men approached and blocked her path. They asked if she had any weapons. Dorothy claimed that her only weapon was her Bible. She then proceeded to read from the Beatitudes in Matthew 5. Before she could finish, though, the men fired several shots into Dorothy's body and head, killing her on the spot.

After her death, Dorothy received many honors for her life and legacy, including recognition by the U.S. Congress, several colleges and universities, and even the

AN EARTHY SPIRITUALITY

Isidore saw work as an opportunity for prayer, often conversing with God
and the saints while tending the fields. And he saw farming as a way to steward God's natural gifts and share them with people in need. The earth was
made for man, as indeed Isidore knew, but not just for *one* man — for all of
them.

Miracles highlighting this special relationship to the earth marked
Isidore's life. For example, one snowy day, he went with his coworkers to a
mill in order to grind a large bag of corn. Along the way, they passed a flock
of pigeons pecking on the frosty ground, vainly searching for food. Taking
pity on the poor birds, Isidore leaned down and poured half his sack of corn
onto the ground. His coworkers initially mocked and chastised him. But
they stopped berating him upon arriving at the mill, when they discovered
that Isidore's bag was completely full. Even more, tradition holds that when
Isidore ground the corn, it produced double the usual amount of flour.

Whether true or not, this strange episode illustrates what Fr. Robert
Barron calls the "loop of grace"[175] — that gratuitous, superabundant giving
that multiplies upon itself. When we properly care for creation, God's earth
responds with copious fruit, both literally and figuratively.

Another episode points to Isidore's earthy spirituality. According to tradition, his master once expressed great thirst and asked Isidore to find him
some water. But the request came in the middle of summer, when the land
was extremely dry, and Isidore knew the nearest river flowed miles away. So
he knelt on the ground and prayed. Almost immediately, a fountain of fresh
water burst forth from the earth and Isidore filled up a cup for his master.

Isidore died in 1130, several years before his wife. Almost 500 years later,
on March 12, 1622, Pope Gregory XV celebrated what may have been the
most prestigious canonization ceremony in Church history. It included four
spiritual giants: St. Ignatius of Loyola, St. Francis Xavier, St. Teresa of Ávila,
and St. Philip Neri. Yet alongside those saints the Pope canonized the simple,
pious farmer, Isidore. His popularity surged after his canonization, spreading
even further around the world. Today, he's venerated as the patron saint of
farmers, peasants, brick layers, and laborers, and several Spanish cities hon-

or him as their patron including Madrid, Leon, and Saragossa.

LESSONS FROM ST. ISIDORE THE FARMER

Isidore's life as a holy farmer offers us at least three different lessons concerning care for creation. First, he highlights the connection between the environment and the poor. We know from recent history that environmental catastrophes, whether they be natural or man-made, tend to disproportionately harm the poor. From typhoons and tsunamis to oil leaks and deforesting, when the natural world is harmed, poor families often lose their homes, their food, or their sources of income.

The Church constantly frames care for creation as a justice issue. The *Compendium of the Social Doctrine of the Church* states that, "Care for the environment … is a matter of a common and universal duty, that of respecting a common good."[176] Isidore knew that when he farmed the land, or ground his grain, it was for the benefit of the general community — his master and himself, indeed, but also the poor, who had no means to procure food. Thus, the environment became for him a gift to steward and an aid to the common good.

Second, Isidore demonstrates how to properly cultivate the earth. In the book of Genesis, God places man and woman on earth to care for and cultivate creation (Gn 2:15). But what does this entail? Pope Francis explains: "To cultivate reminds me of the care that the farmer has for his land so that it bears fruit, and it is shared: how much attention, passion, and dedication!"[177]

THE DUTY OF CARING FOR ANIMALS

"Animals, like plants and inanimate beings, are by nature destined for the common good of past, present, and future humanity. Use of the mineral, vegetable, and animal resources of the universe cannot be divorced from respect for moral imperatives. Man's dominion over inanimate and other living beings granted by the Creator is not absolute; it is limited by concern for the quality of life of his neighbor, including generations to come; it requires a religious respect for the integrity of creation.

"Animals are God's creatures. He surrounds them with his providential care. By their mere existence they bless him and give him glory. Thus men owe them kindness. We should recall the gentleness with which saints like St. Francis of Assisi or St. Philip Neri treated animals. God entrusted animals to the stewardship of those whom he created in his own image."

— *Catechism of the Catholic Church*, 2415–2417

Isidore embodied these traits. He farmed the land with care and intention instead of exploiting it for mere profit.

The "care and cultivation" enjoined in Genesis require us to grasp the rhythm and logic of creation. But we can't do that, Pope Francis argues, if we are "driven by [the] pride of domination, of possessions, manipulation, of exploitation." When these desires overtake us, "we do not care for [creation], we do not respect it, we do not consider it as a free gift that we must care for."[178] By living and farming within this rhythm, Isidore developed an attitude of wonder, contemplation, and solidarity with creation, and it's why the Church has chosen him the patron of farmers.

Third, Isidore shows that our stewardship should be gentle and tender, much like we would treat a child. We see that in the ways Isidore cared for his animal friends and the way he plowed his master's land. During his installation homily, Pope Francis encouraged a similar attitude: "Here I would add one more thing: caring, protecting, demands goodness, it calls for a certain tenderness.... [Tenderness] is not the virtue of the weak but rather a sign of strength of spirit and a capacity for concern, for compassion, for genuine openness to others, for love. We must not be afraid of goodness, of tenderness!"[179]

"No one must say that they cannot be close to the poor because their own lifestyle demands more attention to other areas. This is an excuse commonly heard in academic, business or professional, and even ecclesial circles. While it is quite true that the essential vocation and mission of the lay faithful is to strive that earthly realities and all human activity may be transformed by the Gospel, none of us can think we are exempt from concern for the poor and for social justice."

— Pope Francis[180]

Compendium of the Social Doctrine of the Church (USCCB Publishing, 2005), by Pontifical Council for Justice and Peace

Catholic Social Thought: The Documentary Heritage (Orbis, 2010), edited by David J. O'Brien and Thomas A. Shannon

A Concise Guide to Catholic Social Teaching (Ave Maria, 2013), by Kevin E. McKenna

The Social Doctrine of the Church (Midwest Theological Forum, 2013), by Mike Aquilina

Catholic Social Teaching: Our Best Kept Secret (Orbis, 2003), by Edward P. DeBerri and James E. Hug

Catholic Social Teaching: Learning and Living Justice (Ave Maria, 2007), by Michael Pennock

ACKNOWLEDGMENTS

First and foremost, thanks to Bert Ghezzi, my patient editor and closest friend. By co-teaching the "Saints and Social Justice" course at St. Mary Magdalen and believing in this project from beginning to end, you deserve so much credit. Thanks for being my Samwise.

I must also thank Greg Erlandson and the Our Sunday Visitor team for once again trusting a young author and for producing a stellar book. You're a super talented group and a joy to work with.

Thanks to Fr. Jim Martin, Tom Neal, Matthew Bunson, and Thomas Craughwell for your many suggestions and feedback. Your fingerprints are all over this book. I'm especially grateful to Wanda Gawronska and Archbishop Peter Sartain for your helpful suggestions regarding Bl. Pier Giorgio Frassati.

Thanks to my friends at Word on Fire for your enthusiasm, support, and friendship, particularly Fr. Steve Grunow, my spiritual wellspring, and Fr. Robert Barron, my inspiration and great hero. You two continue pushing me to greater heights.

This book would not have been possible without the love and sacrifice of my family. To all the parents, grandparents, brothers, and sisters, thanks for your encouragement and timely babysitting. To my dear children, I'm so grateful you let Daddy slip away for a few weekend hours to work on the book. I love you.

Most of all, thanks to my dearest Kathleen, my bride, my source, my best friend, and my joy. Without you, this adventure never would have happened. Thank for you for your relentless encouragement, many sacrifices, and tireless care. You're a saint and my real guide to changing the world.

To Pope Francis, our Holy Father: you embody the themes in this book. Thanks for your compelling witness, your remarkable charity, and your zeal for growing a "poor Church for the poor." This book easily could have been about you.

To all the saintly heroes featured within, who journeyed with me and prayed for me throughout this process, I'm so grateful for your friendship. You changed and continue to change the world — especially mine.

And to the Father, Son, and Holy Spirit: all glory be to you as it was in the beginning, is now, and ever shall be, world without end. Amen.

1. Pope Francis, *Evangelii Gaudium*, 183.

2. Glenn Beck, quoted in "Glenn Beck: 'Leave Your Church,'" *Christianity Today*, March 12, 2010. Accessed online at www.christianitytoday.com/ct/2010/marchweb-only/20-51.0.html.

3. Fr. Charles Fell, quoted in Peter Doyle, "Charles Fell, Miracles, and the Lives of Saints," in *Analecta Bollandiana* 119, June 2001.

4. Pope Francis, *Evangelii Gaudium*, 201.

5. Pope Paul VI, *Evangelii Nuntiandi*, 41.

6. United States Conference of Catholic Bishops, *Sharing Catholic Social Teaching: Challenges and Directions* (Washington, DC: USCCB, 1998).

7. Quoted in Jim Forest, "Dorothy Day, Saint and Troublemaker," *Casa Maria Catholic Worker House*. Accessed online at www.lovingjustwise.com/new_page_124.htm.

8. Mother Teresa, *Loving Jesus* (Cincinnati: Servant Books, 1991), p. 112.

9. www.gallup.com/poll/3367/mother-teresa-voted-american-people-most-admired-person-century.aspx.

10. *YOUCAT*, edited by Cardinal Christoph Schonborn (San Francisco, CA: Ignatius Press, 2011), 280.

11. Malcolm Muggeridge, *Something Beautiful for God* (London: Collins Clear Type Press, 1971), pp. 74-75.

12. Leo Maasburg, *Mother Teresa of Calcutta: A Personal Portrait* (San Francisco: Ignatius Press, 2011), p.79.

13. Mother Teresa, *Loving Jesus* (Cincinnati, OH: Servant Books, 1991), p. 21.

14. Mother Teresa, ed. by Jose Luis Gonzáles-Balado, *One Heart Full of Love* (Cincinnati, OH: Servant Books, 1988), p. 7.

15. Quoted in Malcolm Muggeridge, *Something Beautiful for God* (London, England: Collins Clear Type Press, 1971), p. 119.

16. Mother Teresa, *Loving Jesus* (Cincinnati, OH: Servant Books, 1991), p. 112.

17. Mother Teresa, speech at the National Prayer Breakfast, February 5, 1994.

18. Dr. Seuss, *Horton Hears a Who!* (New York, NY: Random House, 1954), p. 47.

19. Quoted in James Martin, *My Life With the Saints* (Chicago, IL: Loyola Press, 2006), p. 169.

20. James Martin, SJ, "The Catholic Brothers and St. Alphonsus Rodriguez," *America*, October 28, 2010.

21. John L. Allen, Jr., "Pope Francis Gets His 'Oxygen' from the Slums." *National Catholic Reporter*, April 7, 2013.

22. Roman Office of Readings, September 9.

23. Pope John Paul II, *Centesimus Annus* ("The Hundredth Year"), #11.

24. Arnold Lunn, "A Saint in the Slave Trade," from John Chapin, *A Treasury of Catholic Reading* (New York: Farrar, Straus and Cudahy, 1957).

25. Alban Butler, *Butler's Lives of the Saints: New Full Edition; September*, ed. David Hugh Farmer, (Collegeville, MN: The Liturgical Press, 1997), p. 79.

26. Ibid., pp.79-80.

27. "The Friendship," in *The Guideposts Treasury of Love* (New York: Bantam, 1982), p. 261.

28. "The Shackles of Slavery in Niger," *ABC News*, June 3, 2005, abcnews.go .com/Nightline/story?id=813618&page=1.

29. "World Reaches Historic Record of 27 Million Slaves, Says Jada Pinkett Smith," *CNS News*, July 17, 2012, cnsnews.com/news/article/world-reaches-historic-record-27-million-slaves-says-jada-pinkett-smith.

30. USCCB. "Anti-Trafficking Program." Anti-Trafficking Program. N.p., n.d. Web. 19 June 2013. www.usccb.org/about/anti-trafficking-program/.

31. United States Conference of Catholic Bishops, *Sharing Catholic Social Teaching: Challenges and Directions* (Washington, DC: USCCB, 1998).

32. www.catholic.org/saints/saint.php?saint_id=49.

33. Alban Butler, *Vol. 1: The Lives of the Fathers, Martyrs and Other Principal Saints* (New York: P. J. Kenedy, 1903), p. 551.

34. Quoted in Bert Ghezzi, *Voices of the Saints* (Chicago, IL: Loyola Press, 2009), pp. 436-437.

35. Quotes online at www.catholic.org/saints/saint.php?saint_id=49.

36. Alban Butler, *Butler's Lives of the Saints: New Full Edition; March*, ed. David Hugh Farmer, (Collegeville, MN: The Liturgical Press, 1999), p.82.

37. Pope John Paul II, Homily at Apostolic Visit to Australia, November 30, 1986.

38. Michael Richardson, *The Adventurous Nun: The Story of Anne-Marie Javouhey*, Australian Catholic Truth Society, No. 1467 (1965).

39. Ibid.

40. Alban Butler, *Butler's Lives of the Saints: New Full Edition; July*, ed. David Hugh Farmer, (Collegeville, MN: The Liturgical Press, 1997), p. 124.

41. Michael Richardson, *The Adventurous Nun: The Story of Anne-Marie Javouhey*, Australian Catholic Truth Society, No. 1467 (1965).

42. Ibid.

43. Ibid.

44. *Forming Consciences for Faithful Citizenship*, #13.

45. Bert Ghezzi, *Voices of the Saints* (Chicago, IL: Loyola Press, 2009), p. 536.

46. Alban Butler, *Butler's Lives of the Saints: New Full Edition; November*, ed. David Hugh Farmer, (Collegeville, MN: The Liturgical Press, 1997), p. 126.

47. C.J. McNaspy, *Conquistador without a Sword: The Life of Roque González, S.J.* (Chicago, IL: Loyola Press, 1982), pp. 93-95.

48. Alban Butler, *Butler's Lives of the Saints: New Full Edition; November*, ed. David Hugh Farmer, (Collegeville, MN: The Liturgical Press, 1997), p. 126.

49. Pope John Paul II, *Christifideles Laici*, 38.

50. St. Gianna Beretta Molla, *Love Letters to My Husband* (Boston, MA: Pauline Books & Media, 2002), p. 14.

51. C. J. McNaspy, S.J. and J.M. Blanch, S.J., *Lost Cities of Paraguay* (Chicago, IL: Loyola University Press, 1982), p. 197.

52. Ibid., 10.

53. Alban Butler, *Butler's Lives of the Saints: New Full Edition; November*, ed. David Hugh Farmer, (Collegeville, MN: The Liturgical Press, 1997), p. 127.

54. Martin Luther King, Jr., *A Knock at Midnight: Inspiration from the Great Sermons of Reverend Martin Luther King, Jr.* (New York: Warner Books, 1998).

55. Elizabeth M. Ince, *St. Thomas More of London* (San Francisco, CA, Ignatius Press, 2003), pp. 15-17.

56. Ibid., pp. 18-19.

57. Ibid., pp. 20-21.

58. www.catholicculture.org/news/features/index.cfm?recnum=6254.

59. Alban Butler, *Butler's Lives of the Saints: New Full Edition; June*, ed. David Hugh Farmer, (Collegeville, MN: The Liturgical Press, 1997), p. 168.

60. Elizabeth M. Ince, *St. Thomas More of London* (San Francisco, CA: Ignatius Press, 2003), p. 136.

61. Ibid., pp. 138-139.

62. Ibid., p. 157.

63. Ibid., p. 160.

64. Ibid., p. 160.

65. Alban Butler, *Butler's Lives of the Saints: New Full Edition; June*, ed. David Hugh Farmer, (Collegeville, MN: The Liturgical Press, 1997), p. 169.

66. United States Conference of Catholic Bishops, *Sharing Catholic Social Teaching: Challenges and Directions* (Washington, DC: USCCB, 1998).

67. St. Basil the Great, *Homilia in illud dictum evangelii secundum Lucam: «Destruam horrea mea, et majora ædificabo:» itemque de avaritia* (Homily on the saying of the *Gospel According to Luke*, "I will pull down my barns and build bigger ones," and on greed), §7.

68. Luciana Frassati, *A Man of the Beatitudes: Pier Giorgio Frassati* (San Francisco, CA: Ignatius Press, 1993), p. 21.

69. Ibid., p. 22.

70. Ibid., p. 93.

71. Ibid., p. 133.

72. Robert Claude, *The Soul of Pier-Giorgio Frassati*, trans. Una Morrissy (New York, NY: Spiritual Book Associates, 1960), pp. 16-17.

73. Ibid., pp. 35-36.

74. John Zmirak, "The Wild One: Blessed Pier Giorgio," *Faith & Family* magazine, February 2001.

75. Quoted in Maria Di Lorenzo, *Blessed Pier Giorgio Frassati: An Ordinary Christian*, trans. Robert Ventresca (Boston, MA: Pauline Books & Media, 2004), p. 73.

76. Luciana Frassati, *A Man of the Beatitudes: Pier Giorgio Frassati* (San Francisco, CA: Ignatius Press, 1993), p. 11.

77. Ibid., p. 44.

78. Bert Ghezzi, *Saints at Heart: How Fault-Filled, Problem-Prone People Like Us Can Be Holy* (Chicago, IL: Loyola Press, 2007), p. 133.

79. Maria Di Lorenzo, *Blessed Pier Giorgio Frassati: An Ordinary Christian*, trans. Robert Ventresca (Boston, MA: Pauline Books & Media, 2004), pp. 59-60.

80. Ibid., p. 81.

81. Ibid.

82. Ibid., p. 72.

83. Quoted in John Zmirak, "The Wild One: Blessed Pier Giorgio," *Faith & Family* magazine, February 2001.

84. Quoted in Bert Ghezzi, *Saints at Heart: How Fault-Filled, Problem-Prone People Like Us Can Be Holy* (Chicago, IL: Loyola Press, 2007), p. 132.

85. Shane Claiborne, *The Irresistible Revolution: Living as an Ordinary Radical* (Grand Rapids, MI: Zondervan, 2006), pp. 113-14.

86. Quoted at www.seton.net/about_seton/setons_history_and_heritage/st_vincent_de_paul/.

87. Interview with John Allen, Jr., *National Catholic Reporter*, July 19, 2011. Accessed online at ncronline.org/news/people/exclusive-interview-archbishop-charles-chaput.

88. Quoted in Bert Ghezzi, *Voices of the Saints* (New York: Doubleday, 2000), p. 244-245.

89. Alban Butler, *Butler's Lives of the Saints: New Full Edition; September*, ed. David Hugh Farmer, (Collegeville, Minnesota: The Liturgical Press, 1999), p. 251.

90. Ibid.

91. Antoine Dégert, "St. Vincent de Paul," *The Catholic Encyclopedia. Vol. 15* (New York: Robert Appleton Company, 1912).

92. Jim Forest, "What I Learned About Justice from Dorothy Day," *Salt of the Earth*, July-August 1995. Accessed online at www.uscatholic.org/culture/social-justice/2009/02/what-i-learned-about-justice-dorothy-day.

93. Antoine Dégert, "St. Vincent de Paul," *The Catholic Encyclopedia. Vol. 15* (New York: Robert Appleton Company, 1912).

94. Ibid.

95. Ibid.

96. Alban Butler, *Butler's Lives of the Saints: New Full Edition; September*, ed. David Hugh Farmer, (Collegeville, Minnesota: The Liturgical Press, 1999), p. 252.

97. Antoine Dégert, "St. Vincent de Paul," *The Catholic Encyclopedia. Vol. 15* (New York: Robert Appleton Company, 1912).

98. Quoted at www.holyspiritinteractive.net/kids/saints/0927_vincent.asp.

99. United States Conference of Catholic Bishops, *Sharing Catholic Social Teaching: Challenges and Directions* (Washington, DC: USCCB, 1998).

100. Gregory the Great, *Dialogues*, 1.

101. Pope Pius XII, *Fulgens Radiatur*, 9.

102. *Lives of the Saints*, "St. Benedict of Nursia," edited by Father Joseph Vann (New York: John J. Crawley, 1954).

103. Pius XII, *Fulgens Radiatur*, 11.

104. Ibid., 12.

105. Brother Lawrence, *The Practice of the Presence of God* (New York: Wilder Publications, 2008), p. 21.

106. Ibid., p. 22.

107. Benedict of Nursia, *The Rule of St. Benedict in English* (Collegeville, MN: The Liturgical Press, 1981) p. 69.

108. Benedict of Nursia, *The Holy Rule* (London: Thomas Richardson and Son, 1865), pp. 72.

109. Ibid., p. 105.

110. Benedict of Nursia, *The Rule of St. Benedict in English* (Collegeville, MN: The Liturgical Press, 1981) p. 70.

111. Accessed at www.catholicculture.org/culture/liturgicalyear/calendar/day.cfm?date=2013-05-01.

112. *Lives of the Saints*, edited by Father Joseph Vann (New York: John J. Crawley, 1954).

113. Pope Pius XII, *Fulgens Radiatur*, 18.

114. Josemaría Escrivá, *Friends of God* (New York: Scepter Publishers, 2002), p. 78.

115. Josemaría Escrivá, *The Way* (New York: Image Books, 2006), p. 143.

116. Josemaría Escrivá, *Christ is Passing By* (New York: Scepter Publishers, 1974), p. 107.

117. Pope Pius XII, *Fulgens Radiatur* (Encyclical on St. Benedict), 29.

118. Pope Francis, Homily on Labor Day, May 1, 2013.

119. Pope John Paul II, *Laborem Exercens (On Human Work)*, 9.

120. Quoted in Sharon Otterman, "In Hero of the Catholic Left, a Conservative Cardinal Sees a Saint," *New York Times*, November 27, 2012.

121. Quoted in Otterman.

122. Jim Forest, "The living legacy of Dorothy Day," salt.claretianpubs.org/issues/DorothyDay/legacy.html.

123. Dorothy Day, *The Long Loneliness* (New York: Harper Collins, 1996), p. 25.

124. Ibid., p. 38.

125. Jim Forest, "Catholic Worker Movement" in Michael Glazier, *The Encyclopedia of American Catholic History* (Collegeville, MN: Liturgical Press, 1997).

126. Dorothy Day, *The Long Loneliness* (New York: Harper Collins, 1996), p. 150.

127. Ibid., pp. 135-136.

128. Quoted by Jim Forest, "Catholic Worker Movement" in Michael Glazier, *The Encyclopedia of American Catholic History* (Collegeville, MN: Liturgical Press, 1997).

129. Quoted in Jim Forest, "The living legacy of Dorothy Day," salt.claretianpubs.org/issues/DorothyDay/legacy.html.

130. Dorothy Day, *The Long Loneliness* (New York: Harper Collins, 1996), p. 166.

131. Quoted in Jim Forest, *Love is the Measure: A Biography of Dorothy Day* (Maryknoll, NY: Orbis Books, 2002), p.56.

132. Quoted in Jim Forest, "The living legacy of Dorothy Day," salt .claretianpubs.org/issues/DorothyDay/legacy.html.

133. See David L. Gregory, "Dorothy Day, Workers' Rights, and Catholic Authenticity," *Fordham Urban Law Journal*, Volume 26, Issue 5 (1998). Accessed online at ir.lawnet.fordham.edu/cgi/viewcontent.cgi?article=1760&context=ulj.

134. Ibid.

135. Dorothy Day, "Love is the Measure," *The Catholic Worker*, June 1942.

136. According to 2013 CARA data, which shows 1,188,836 religious and 1.196 billion Catholics in the world. cara.georgetown.edu/CARAServices/ requestedchurchstats.html.

137. Second Vatican Council, *Lumen Gentium*, 31.

138. Quoted by Jim Forest, "Catholic Worker Movement" in Michael Glazier, *The Encyclopedia of American Catholic History* (Collegeville, MN: Liturgical Press, 1997).

139. United States Conference of Catholic Bishops, *Sharing Catholic Social Teaching: Challenges and Directions* (Washington, DC: USCCB, 1998).

140. Edward Stourton, *John Paul II: Man of History* (London: Hodd & Stoughton, 2006), p. 60.

141. Pope Francis, speech on July 25, 2013. Accessed online at *America* magazine.org/content/all-things/pope-among-poor-speaks-social-justice.

142. Accessed online at www.local-life.com/gdansk/articles/solidarity.

143. Quoted at education-for-solidarity.blogspot.com/2011/05/maximilian-kolbe.html.

144. Ibid.

145. Quoted in Carl Bernstein, "The Holy Alliance," *Time* magazine, February 24, 1992. Accessed online at www.carlbernstein.com/magazine_holy_alliance.php.

146. Catholic Herald Staff, "John Paul II: His Dramatic Life Story," *The Catholic Herald*, January 12, 2011. Accessed online at www.catholicherald.co.uk/ features/2011/01/12/john-paul-ii-his-dramatic-life-story/.

147. Ryan Chilcote, "Gorbachev: Pope was 'example to all of us,'" CNN.com, April 4, 2005. Accessed online at www.cnn.com/2005/WORLD/europe/04/03/pope .gorbachev/.

148. Pope Benedict XVI, *Caritas in Veritate*, 58.

149. "Final days, last words of Pope John Paul II," Catholic World News, September 20, 2005. Accessed online at www.catholicculture.org/news/features/index.cfm?recnum=39699.

150. United States Conference of Catholic Bishops, *Called To Global Solidarity International Challenges For U.S. Parishes* (Washington, DC: USCCB, 1997).

151. Pope John Paul II, *Centesimus Annus*, 51.

152. United States Conference of Catholic Bishops, *Called To Global Solidarity International Challenges For U.S. Parishes* (Washington, DC: USCCB, 1997).

153. Pope John Paul II, *Sollicitudo rei Socialis*, 38.

154. Edward W. Desmond, "Interview with Mother Teresa: A Pencil in the Hand of God," *Time* magazine, December 4, 1989.

155. Quoted in Charles Paulino, *L'Osservatore Romano* (English Edition), "A Missionary Unafraid to Live and Die with His People," October 14, 2009.

156. Fulton Sheen, *Treasure in Clay: The Autobiography of Fulton J. Sheen* (New York: Image Books, 1982), pp. 120-121.

157. Quoted in Franciscans of St. Anthony's Guild, "Damien the Leper" (Patterson, New Jersey: 1974). Access online at www.ewtn.com/library/MARY/DAMIEN.HTM.

158. Ibid.

159. Quoted in Charles Paulino, *L'Osservatore Romano* (English Edition), "A Missionary Unafraid to Live and Die with His People," October 14, 2009.

160. Ibid.

161. Ibid.

162. Ibid.

163. Quoted by Rev. Daren J. Zehnle, K.H.S., "Blessed Damien quotes," *Servant and Steward*. Accessed online at dzehnle.blogspot.com/2009/02/blessed-damien-quotes.html.

164. United States Conference of Catholic Bishops, *Sharing Catholic Social Teaching: Challenges and Directions* (Washington, DC: USCCB, 1998).

165. Amy Steedman, *I God's Garden* (Toronto: Morang & Company, LTD, 1906), p. 80.

166. *YOUCAT*, edited by Cardinal Christoph Schonborn (San Francisco, CA: Ignatius Press, 2011), 280.

167. William L. Patenaude, "St. Giles: A Seventh-Century Catholic Ecologist," Catholic Ecology Blog, Accessed online at catholicecology.blogspot.com/2012/06/st-giles-seventh-century-catholic.html.

168. Thomas E. Woods, Jr., *How the Catholic Church Built Western Civilization* (Washington, D.C.: Regnery Publishing, 2005), p. 29.

169. Ibid.

170. Ibid., 31.

171. Pope Benedict XVI, General Audience on August 26, 2009.

172. Pope Benedict XVI, Message for "Save Creation Day" on September 1, 2007.

173. Pope Francis, Installation Homily on Solemnity of St. Joseph, March 19, 2013.

174. Quoted by Fr. Richard Butler, "St. Isidore the Farmer," Church of St. Isidore. Accessed online at www.stisidorestow.org/About/stIsidore.html.

175. Robert Barron, "The Loop of Grace," Sermon on July 31, 2005. Accessed online at www.wordonfire.org/WOF-Radio/Sermons/2005/Sermon-238---18th-Sunday-in-Ordinary-Time----The-L.aspx.

176. *Compendium of the Social Doctrine of the Church*, 466.

177. Pope Francis, Homily on World Environment Day, June 5, 2013.

178. Ibid.

179. Pope Francis, Installation Homily on Solemnity of St. Joseph, March 19, 2013.

180. Pope Francis, *Evangelii Gaudium*, 201.